Better Together. Crossing the Divide in South Africa.
Published in South Africa. Copyright Roger Pearce © 2016.
ISBN 978-0-620-72354-1

In most instances the English Standard Version of the Bible was quoted.

Book design by Lionheart Ink.™

BETTER TOGETHER

CROSSING THE DIVIDE
IN SOUTH AFRICA

ROGER PEARCE

CONTRIBUTORS: MOSS NTLHA, SIMON LEREFOLO, GILIAN & VANESSA DAVIDS, SIVIWE NOTSHE, DERRICK & PRISCILLA MOODLEY, BONGIWE MKHIZE, WILLEM NEL, SERGE SOLOMONS, THOBEKILE SHANGE, JESSE SMITH, DENNIS & NICKY NEVILLE, SHAUN PEARCE, THANDO PHELLO.

EDITOR: **NICKY NEVILLE**

COURT
NEX

1898

I dedicate this book to the people of South Africa, to every tribe and tongue, and to the healing of our nation.

THANK YOU.

I would like to thank the many people who have made this book happen. Thank you to the contributors who shared their hearts, their life stories: Simon Lerefolo, Gilian and Vanessa Davids, Willem Nel, Siviwe Notshe, Derrick and Priscilla Moodley, Serge Solomons, Bongiwe Mkhize, Thobekile Shange, Jesse Smith, Shaun Pearce and Thando Phello. Thank you to Dennis and Nicky Neville for co-writing some of the chapters in the book. Thank you to Lynne van Coller for her poem, *Dunoon*.

I would also like to give me sincere thanks to Rev. Moss Ntlha for his foreword, which was a great encouragement to me.

A heartfelt thank you to Nicky Neville who was instrumental in putting the book together and for her writing and editing skills. Thank you to the proof readers Christelle van Wyk, Daniella Neville, Joanne Pardey and Sherry Neville.

I would like to give a special thanks to Tracie du Toit for the beautiful design of this book. My gratitude also goes to the photographers who contributed their beautiful photos: Star & Harbour Photography, Talitha Neville, AlexanderSmith Photography, Sherry Neville, Charles Hellyar, Rochelle Fouché from Hannah Blue and Samantha Jackson Photography.

Thank you to my beautiful wife, Nicola, for her prayers, support and encouragement and to my two sons, James and Shaun. You inspire me.

Most of all, thank you to my Lord and Saviour, the Lover of my soul, the Lord Jesus Christ. In Him, all things are possible.

Thank you.

FOREWORD

REV. MOSS NTLHA

GENERAL SECRETARY OF THE
EVANGELICAL ALLIANCE OF SOUTH AFRICA

For centuries the story of South Africa could not be told without reference to race, along with its two cousins of tribe and class. The colonial history of our nation, followed in 1948 by Apartheid as a system of ordering society, ensured that racism is a foundational fault-line in the nation. To use biblical language, racism became our national idolatry. Much pain and suffering went into the Struggle to dismantle race as a basis for ordering our national life. The father of the South African nation, Nelson Mandela, is a symbol of how much sacrifice South Africans had to make to end racism. At his trial before being sentenced for life imprisonment on Robben Island, Mandela put it this way:

"During my lifetime I have dedicated myself to this struggle of the African people. I have fought against white domination, and I have fought against black domination. I have cherished the ideal of a democratic and free society in which all persons live together in harmony and with equal opportunities. It is an ideal which I hope to live for and to achieve. But if needs be, it is an ideal for which I am prepared to die."

He escaped the gallows by a whisker, and was sentenced to 27 years of incarceration. He was lucky. Some weren't so lucky.

So it was that when the system collapsed in 1994, as a nation we threw away the old Apartheid constitution and set about crafting a new one, acclaimed as one of the most progressive constitutions in the world. Having sorted out the constitutional and legislative paperwork of how we were to live together as South Africans, we forgot an important detail: that we changed the laws of the land and not the people of the land. For the most part, they were still the same people, holding on to their traditional ideologies and worldviews. We were un-transformed. Even the Truth and Reconciliation Committee did not attempt to transform anyone, only dispense amnesty to those who agreed to disclose their crimes. Remorse for one's racist deeds was not even a requirement for amnesty. Only full disclosure. For the most part, racism went underground, only coming up for air every now and then in the post-1994 era. Generally, it continued undetected and causing damage to its victims, who were often told to "forget the past, and stop making race an issue".

It is this background that makes Roger's book brilliant. I know of hardly any intervention in the church community in South Africa today that intentionally confronts the enduring sin of racism, as a key discipleship issue, as Roger's book does. The book is a collage of amazing testimonies regarding the continuously progressing battle fought by the His People/Every Nation community in South Africa to dismantle racism. It is an honest account of ongoing life-on-life discipleship. Unassuming and hard hitting, it unmasks the deceitfulness and self-justification of racism, submitting it to the rigours of God's Word, in the safe spaces of a loving and committed Christian community.

In focussing the search light of Scripture on the foundational sin of our nation, Roger deploys one of the most powerful weapons available to the Christian world to a rather stubborn demon in our national life. There are no slogans, philosophical arguments or worn-out rhetoric in the book. For that, one must look elsewhere. This is rather a book about ordinary folk wrestling before a holy God with the sin of their nation and putting their lives on the line. In this way they have become witnesses, not in words only, but in their daily lives, of the efficacy of the Christian faith to save and redeem us from the tragedy of racism.

This is all the more important because the Christian Bible has a sad history in South Africa. It was misused by the architects of Apartheid to give theological legitimacy to a system that was condemned by the whole world, via the United Nations, as a crime against humanity. A case could be made that as the dust settled following the collapse of Apartheid, many Christians held on to their Bibles rather lightly. When your sacred text stands accused of having allowed itself to be used to justify Apartheid, you can't but suffer a measure of inferiority complex, a loss of nerve in affirming the verities of Scripture too loudly, lest you be reminded by the enemies of Christ of what Christians did in the Apartheid years. We owe a debt of gratitude to Roger for suggesting some of the ways we might reclaim the integrity of the Bible as a resource for battle-weary South Africans. *Better Together* brings fresh energy to the task of contextualising the Gospel in post-Apartheid South Africa. It calls us all to let go of our tribal comfort zones, the ideological bondages of our past, in order to embrace the new thing that God is doing in our nation.

While *Better Together* is an inspiring status report in the journey of the His People/Every Nation Christian community, it is well worth a read for the broader Christian community looking for tools and case studies to help engage the challenges of racism, xenophobia and otherness. It promises valuable nuggets for how we can be intentional about commending Jesus to a world that has become cynical about the claims of the Gospel.

If racial reconciliation and human solidarity were some of the things God hoped to see when He blessed South Africa with the miracle of 1994, *Better Together* gives us helpful pointers about how the church can reignite that dream. What else but the Gospel of Jesus Christ could mount a credible approach toward uprooting the scourge that has plagued South Africa for centuries?

Moss Ntlha is a pastor and leader with extensive experience in serving churches in their search for unity and their mission to proclaim the Gospel. His passion is to see the Gospel of Jesus Christ being truly good news to the poor. This passion is embodied in his pastoral practice, where he is involved in church planting, especially among poor communities. As an activist, he was one of the leading evangelical voices against Apartheid and continues to serve the evangelical cause in post-Apartheid South Africa. Through the Evangelical Alliance of South Africa, where he is the General Secretary, he is involved in public policy advocacy, nationally and internationally. He works ecumenically to sustain a prophetic witness that enables the voice of the poor to be heard in the corridors of power.

CONTENTS

CHAPTER ONE

PULLED AWAY FROM THE KHAYA

ROGER PEARCE

⟫⟶

"To be loved but not known is comforting but superficial. To be known and not loved is our greatest fear. But to be fully known and truly loved is, well, a lot like being loved by God. It is what we need more than anything. It liberates us from pretence, humbles us out of our self-righteousness, and fortifies us for any difficulty life can throw at us."

Timothy Keller

The smell of a fire and pap (maize meal) and sitting outside as the sun sets, surrounded by people and chickens and hearing a language that wasn't mine but becoming familiar, is one of my earliest memories.

I grew up on what was then a small farm on the outskirts of Johannesburg. We used to grow vegetables and fruit to take to the market. About 100 meters from our farm house lived John and his family. He was a farm labourer on our smallholding.

Some of my earliest memories are of hanging out and playing with my friends at John's very modest home, which they referred to as a khaya. I loved their language and I remember feeling so safe there. I felt a level of deep contentment and a feeling of being received. To this day, I love being outdoors when the sun sets and I love the smell of fire and smoke.

Then around 1969 or 1970, when I was 5 or 6 years old, I have a distinct memory of my mom calling me away from the khaya, saying that I could no longer play there, that these people were different from us. I had fantastic parents who loved me dearly, but we lived in the Apartheid era in South Africa at that time, and a young white child just did not hang out at the khaya. I say none of this to dishonour my amazing parents as they too were raised in this system.

I remember suddenly feeling so strange and alienated from my friends at the khaya, like suddenly there was an otherness about them. The thing is that as a young child you don't understand these things. You just trust the input you receive from your parents and the society around you. From that time onwards everything was different. I was pulled away from the khaya and I wish I hadn't been.

WHEN FEAR CAME IN

In 1976, my sisters and I were driving in the back of a car with our Ouma (granny). I was 11 years old and we were listening to a radio broadcast about the Soweto riots taking place. It must have been 16 June. My sisters and I could sense the immense fear in our Ouma on hearing the news; and she suddenly had a real sense of urgency to get us home to safety. That day, driving up Jules Street in her Peugeot 504, her fear and anxiety were somehow passed on to my sisters and I. For years we lived with that sense of danger and mistrust of the "other". We lived with a terrible fear of black people and what the future would hold. I had lived in a safe world before then and all of a sudden that safety was threatened. It took me many years until I could deal with that sense of danger.

THE SOWETO RIOTS

The Soweto riots of 1976 were the most brutal and violent riots that had taken place against the South African Apartheid administration. On 16 June 1976, over 20 000 students turned up to march, followed closely by the police. Conflict began almost immediately and police fired round after round of tear-gas and then guns into the crowds. The police showed no mercy and attacked students of all ages, armed or unarmed.

Hector Pieterson (1964 – June 16, 1976) became the iconic image of the 1976 Soweto Uprising in Apartheid South Africa when a news photograph by Sam Mzima of the dying Hector being carried by a fellow student, was published around the world. He was killed at the age of 12 when the police opened fire on protesting students.[1]

As a teenager, I grew up in the days of the Cold War. It was a bipolar world — the USA/Free World vs the Soviet Union and the 'communist onslaught'. We received propaganda constantly from all media sources and lived in an era of censored press. Our environment was very much controlled all through the 70s and into the 80s. In high school, it was a rite of passage for white young men to register for National Defence Force service at the age of 16. This meant that young men were conscripted into the army. We all had mixed feelings about this legal obligation. We were continuously fed messages of the "Rooi Gevaar" (red danger — a term used for communists).

The Western press reinforced this message, and when Mozambique was liberated, we heard all the stories at school from Portuguese refugees who fled the country, telling us of bloodshed, sisters being raped and horror upon horror. The personal stories reinforced the narrative that we were hearing. We understood that communism was evil and that black people were on the communists' side, making them particularly dangerous.

It is hard to comprehend, but we had no idea that the army was oppressing people in townships. We only knew that they were on the borders fighting off those from the outside who wanted to invade our country. We didn't think we were on the wrong side. The world was a clear place — the West vs the Soviets. We were blind to the oppression that the people around us were living under.

To be honest, I hadn't even heard of Nelson Mandela or the Rivonia Trial or any of these things. All this information was kept from us by the government and media. I know now that in life our experiences, as powerful and as vivid as they are, do not necessarily reflect reality.

TIME FOR A REALITY CHECK

My process of awakening to the reality of what was going on around me began in my final year of school when I had the privilege of having supper with an 80-year old author, Alan Paton, who wrote *Cry The Beloved Country*. His passion for justice in South Africa was evident and one meal with him made a profound impact on my life.

It was during this time that I realised how sick and tired I was of being sick and tired. I'd had enough of compromising, of half following God and half not. I was great at theory, but wasn't living it. I resolved to live the Bible. As God came into my life and started touching my heart, I began a journey of shedding the mind-sets and perspectives of the past. It wasn't one moment of deep revelation that changed me, but rather a slow awakening, like coming out of a deep sleep.

MY JOURNEY OF AWAKENING

I entered into a new season of life, studying to be a Chartered Accountant at the University of the Witwatersrand (Wits) in Johannesburg. There was a library at Wits called the William Cullen Library, which had such a sense of the forbidden, because in it there were books that were banned. I found myself going into this library, reading these books and starting to see things in a different light. I also read about some of the other revolutionary struggles in the world, including the Algerian War and some of the dirty tricks the French employed in that situation[2]. As I was reading about other countries and other revolutionary struggles, I started to see faint innuendos of the same things happening right here. I became more aware of the news and started reading far and wide. I read up on the CCB (the South African Civil Cooperation Bureau — a government-sponsored death squad during the Apartheid era) and it dawned on me that 'my world' was a sanitised version of the real world and that the reality of South Africa was very different from what I thought it was.

One day I found myself in a lecture theatre where a black student society meeting was taking place. At that stage black students didn't participate in any student activities. This was an act of solidarity because they weren't allowed to vote. At first it was ridiculous to me that they didn't participate as I thought this was a place where they had the opportunity to do so, yet as I watched them and listened to them that day, I started understanding why this was important. They were on the outskirts of university life and had no say. Solidarity in itself gave them a voice and allowed them to have an influence.

Another defining moment for me was when Eric Pelser, a friend from school, suddenly disappeared in his second year at Wits. I later heard that he had joined the ANC and the armed struggle. He was actually captured a couple of years later. I was astounded that he would give up his studies and his future for this cause, and this really made me rethink my simplistic, sanitised worldview.

BEING CALLED UP AND OUT

My church at the time was all white and very conservative. At one stage, the broader movement decided to start combining their churches (black and white). Our local church's council, however, opted to leave the movement and continue with their whites-only policy. I remember thinking that it was not right — their decision was saddening to me and I started to disengage from this church. These were the kind of decisions people were making in a response to fear and in an attempt to hold on to what was 'safe'.

A few years later, I had the joy of meeting Maranatha missionaries on Wits campus. Maranatha was an evangelical campus ministry that many of our Every Nation leaders joined in the 80s. We welcomed them onto the campus and so began an incredible journey of finding my spiritual family — finding people who sounded different, but who shared the same heart. They had a profound impact on me because of their passion for discipleship and for dealing with heart issues, making sure that Christ was fully formed in us. As the apostle Paul said in Galatians 4:19: "My little children, of whom I travail in birth again until Christ be formed in you." This was a ministry I wanted to be part of.

I am so thankful for Pastor Bill Bennot, the Senior Pastor of Maranatha, and his impact on my life and for my brothers who helped me as I was coming alive to God. Two men who were the best men at my wedding, Wayne Smith and Rob Stecher, challenged me continuously regarding attitudes and flaws. We were part of a culture where we were constantly calling each other up and out. In retrospect, I realise how much rebellion and selfishness was in me. Having the pastors and my brothers around me, and being part of a culture that was discipleship orientated, was a key part of me growing as a follower of Christ.

FROM A SENSE OF OTHERNESS
TO A SENSE OF SAMENESS

I moved into a guys' commune with my friend, Wayne Smith, and started sharing a room with Eugene Ntshabele, a young black man. At first there was a sense of otherness, and then a sense of sameness. Even seeing someone eating with his hands, was jarring to me. I realised that I had just been conditioned to eat with a knife and fork and I could have been conditioned to eat with chopsticks. Yet, there is a sense of sweet fellowship and intimacy to sharing a meal with somebody in the way they do it in their culture. It's got that biblical component of breaking bread together. There were so many cultural differences we had to overcome, but in the end we realised that we were so alike — he was a great guy with aspirations and values just like mine. We travelled to America together to the Maranatha World Conference in 1989. These were life-changing experiences for me. Between 1992 and 1993, our local Maranatha church joined another South African ministry called His People, and from then on we were called His People throughout South Africa.

One day, I felt led by the Holy Spirit to share the Gospel with people in the canteen at Wits with a loud PA system. Not only was it a privilege to share the Gospel with them, but what a joy it was to meet people from all races and to get insight into their lives and hearts. We all have the same deepest desires; we are all sinful and broken outside of Christ, yet made by God with so much potential. So much of God's gifting

HIS PEOPLE TO EVERY NATION NAME CHANGE

I joined His People Christian Church as a young Christian. Most people who share their stories in this book were part of the His People family in South Africa. This is purely because these are the people I have worked and worshiped with over the years and they have become my family. There are many amazing church movements in our nation and we are honoured to serve alongside them in spreading the Gospel and discipling the nation of South Africa.

In January 2017, most of the His People churches in the Southern African region, will be changing their names to Every Nation. We have, in fact, been part of the Every Nation world-wide family of churches for many years. During a His People Southern Africa leaders meeting in January 2016, we felt the Holy Spirit saying that it was a new season. Out of this came the decision to take on the name Every Nation as a prophetic declaration of inclusion, standing against racism and division in our region. We desire to reach every nation, tribe and tongue with the Gospel of Jesus Christ.

and grace is upon us if we would only realise it. We also used to go door to door at times, sharing the Gospel in a so-called "mixed" area — a neighbourhood where people from all races were living. I met so many people and remember being invited in for a chicken meal. They cooked the chicken in Coke and it was delicious! We also visited some of our church friends in Soweto. At first, my wealthier, white side saw the poverty and how little there was. We were fed a meal and served tea and within an hour did not see anything but their amazing hearts, hospitality and their love for God. The poverty, race and cultural divides just melted away. I saw their love for me and their desire for relationship and didn't see the differences any longer.

On one occasion, we had a cultural evening at church. People came dressed to represent their cultures and we had little food stalls providing their traditional foods. This might sound like nothing, but in those days, before the fall of Apartheid, it was profound. I was at the English stall, serving scones and tea, some friends were at the Afrikaans stall offering biltong (dried and salted meat) and koeksisters (sweet pastries), friends from Ghana had delicious peanut butter and meat soup, and some of our black friends offered us mopane worms (the mopane worm is a delicacy widely consumed in rural areas of South Africa). That was the day I ate my first mopane worm and I must say, I enjoyed it! People from at least twelve different cultural groups shared their culture with each other that day. We ended the evening connecting on a deeper level. In one of the discussions, a black friend from Soweto shared how he felt more connected to Afrikaans people than to English people. He said that he identified with their desire to fight for their

IN 1992, HIS PEOPLE AND MARANATHA HOSTED THE *SYMPOSIUM FOR THE BIBLICAL RECONSTRUCTION OF SOUTH AFRICA* (SYMSA). IT WAS A WATERSHED MOMENT FOR MANY OF US, AS BEFORE WE WERE RAISED ON A DIET OF SEPARATION OF CHURCH AND STATE. SYMSA MADE US REALISE THAT THERE WERE DIFFERENT WAYS OF ENGAGING GOVERNMENT. IT EXPANDED OUR WORLDVIEW AND MADE US REALISE THAT AS CHRISTIANS WE ARE MEANT TO ENGAGE IN ALL SPHERES OF LIFE, INCLUDING GOVERNMENT.

country as it was similar to his motivation in the Struggle. This shattered some of my prideful English liberal perspectives that we were more connected and more empathetic, and so we realised just how complicated this all was. Yet through this all, in God, we started coming together, creating bridges of understanding and unity.

THE SPECKLED BRANCH.

In the early days of His People in South Africa (now called Every Nation in most regions), we had very distinct moments where we apologised and repented for the sins of the past; where we identified times we had made people who weren't white and English, feel alienated. As Apartheid began to break apart and as the harsh realities of what South Africa was really like began to be revealed, we were hit with the ice cold realisation of the hurt that we had inflicted and our own blindness. Raising our sons, James and Shaun, Nicola and I were determined to raise a new generation without the pride and fear of my generation.

We had realised that we needed to talk to each other, we needed to hear each other's stories. Attending racial reconciliation workshops in the church at that time was a major step for all of us in understanding each other. As we listened to each other's stories, it created environments that facilitated repentance and forgiveness and where healing could take place. My journey has been that of multiple conversations, both formal and informal, through which I listened and learnt to understand what other people had been through and what their perspectives were as a result. Breakthroughs came as we all took the time to listen, understand and be vulnerable.

One of the phrases that has become part of the culture in our Johannesburg church, is the 'speckled branch'. This is from the story of Jacob, where he put before the sheep the speckled branch, and whichever of the sheep became speckled, those were his (Genesis 30:25-43). At one stage, we were 90% white, but we would consciously put before the church as much diversity as possible — in the worship team, in those who prayed and preached. It didn't matter which Sunday you came, there would always be a speckled branch. It became part of our lexicon for identity.

We have a huge role to play in helping people cross the divide that still exists in South Africa. At this time, our nation is once again facing serious racial tension; and the Body of Christ is called to rise to the challenge and pray, believe and do something about it. I have a deep conviction that, as Christians, we are not just called to be a prophetic voice in our nation, but that we are called to be a prophetic model.

/ABOUT

Roger and his wife, Nicola, have a passion to see lives transformed through discipleship in the Word, the Presence and the Power of God. They are the Lead Elders of the Every Nation Church in Rosebank (previously called His People), and head up the ten Every Nation congregations in Johannesburg. Roger also leads the Every Nation Apostolic Leadership Team in Africa.

He has a distinct leadership gift and has walked a journey with many churches, teams and companies, helping them overcome relational obstacles and come into their next season. Roger addresses contemporary issues through his bimonthly YouTube video blogs on the Every Nation Southern Africa channel.

Roger and Nicola reside in Johannesburg and have two sons, James and Shaun, who are currently studying at university.

Photo credit: Star & Harbour Photography

APARTHEID

Apartheid was the system of legalised segregation and oppression that divided South African society according to the 'racial group' they belonged to. It came into being after the National Party (NP) came into power in 1948. "Apartheid" is an Afrikaans word that means "separateness" or "the state of being apart". During the Apartheid era, there was a hierarchy of the races. White South Africans were seen as superior to their Black counterparts and, therefore, lived a higher quality life. Black South Africans were oppressed according to the law. Under the Group Areas Act, each racial group was assigned a specific area in which they were allowed to live. This meant that many Coloured, Indian and Black people who were living in what was supposed to be a White area were forcibly removed from their homes and were given inferior housing in their new location. Non-white South Africans had to carry a passbook, which aimed to control their movements outside of their assigned areas. The Bantu Education Act of 1953 further oppressed non-white South Africans as it ensured that the standard of education they received was substandard, which enabled the government to oppress them even further.

A system of oppression is almost certain to result in internal resistance. In South Africa, resistance to Apartheid was initially quite peaceful, with movements such as the Defiance Campaign of the 1950s. The Defiance Campaign consisted of ordinary people purposefully defying "petty Apartheid" laws such as segregation of public transport and even park benches. However, these movements proved ineffective. Uprisings and protests followed and were met with police violence and the imprisonment of anti-Apartheid leaders such as Nelson Mandela. The Struggle, as this resistance movement is called, climaxed in the 1980s as unrest spread and banned political parties such as the African National Congress (ANC), South African Communist Party (SACP) and the Pan Africanist Congress (PAC) began to gain support. External pressure on South Africa for reform, such as sanctions on arms, oil and even sports and culture began to have a negative impact on South Africa's economy and the white mind-set.

F. W. de Klerk became the President of South Africa in September 1989. He began negotiations to end the Apartheid system and, in his parliamentary opening speech on the 2nd of February 1990, he unbanned 33 organisations and announced the release of political prisoners. On the 11th of February 1990, Nelson Mandela was released from prison. This series of events marked a turning point in South Africa's history and led to the nation's first democratic elections on the 27th of April 1994. South Africa then entered a period of reconciliation, specifically in the form of the Truth and Reconciliation Commission, which was chaired by the Archbishop Desmond Tutu and aimed to bring to light the atrocities of Apartheid in order for South African citizens to reconcile. South Africa has been a democratic country for just over twenty years now, but the legacy of Apartheid can still be felt.

THEREFORE, AS YOU RECEIVED CHRIST JESUS THE LORD, SO WALK IN HIM, ROOTED AND BUILT UP IN HIM AND ESTABLISHED IN THE FAITH, JUST AS YOU WERE TAUGHT, ABOUNDING IN THANKSGIVING. SEE TO IT THAT NO ONE TAKES YOU CAPTIVE BY PHILOSOPHY AND EMPTY DECEIT, ACCORDING TO HUMAN TRADITION, ACCORDING TO THE ELEMENTAL SPIRITS OF THE WORLD, AND NOT ACCORDING TO CHRIST.

COLOSSIANS 2:6-8

As you read through the thought-provoking stories in this book, I encourage you to journal about your personal journey and ask the Lord to show you the defining moments in your life that shaped your thinking of people from other races and cultures. There are questions at the end of each chapter to help you in this journey. Prayerfully seek the Lord to show you hurts and misconceptions, unforgiveness and attitudes that might still be influencing your thinking and behaviour. Trust the Lord to set you completely free, once and for all. These questions can also be used in small group settings to help others share their journeys.

JOURNAL POINTS

1. What were the main learning points for you in this chapter?

2. How has history – the story of your people group specifically – shaped your perception of yourself, your people and people from other races or cultural groups?

3. What fears took root in your heart as a child? Have you been able to overcome these fears? If not, commit to finding a way to deal with the fears so that you can be set free.

4. Are you willing to be challenged and to change in the areas of your life that do not align with the truths in God's Word?

5. How do you think you could gain a understanding of people from other races and cultural groups?

Photo credit: Sherry Neville

CHAPTER TWO

WHAT'S YOUR STORY?

ROGER PEARCE

➤——→

"The art of storytelling is your most powerful weapon in the war of ideas."

Carmine Gallo

In the first chapter of this book, I painted a picture of my story. South Africa, however, is a nation with a history — so many different stories that define who we are and how we look at the future. This book is a collection of stories. I have taken the approach of using story as a tool, rather than just writing a textbook on the need for racial reconciliation. This is because stories have tremendous power. The Nigerian poet and novelist, Ben Okri said the following, "Stories can conquer fear, you know. They can make the heart bigger.".

Let's start with the story of a cockroach. "At a restaurant, a cockroach suddenly flew from somewhere and sat on a lady. She started screaming out of fear. With a panic-stricken face and trembling voice, she started jumping, with both her hands desperately trying to get rid of the cockroach. Her reaction was contagious, as everyone in her group also got panicky. The lady finally managed to push the cockroach away ... but it landed on another lady in the group. Now it was the turn of the other lady in the group to continue the drama. The waiter rushed forward to their rescue. In the relay of throwing, the cockroach next fell upon the waiter. The waiter stood firm, composed himself and observed the behaviour of the cockroach on his shirt. When he was confident enough, he grabbed it with his fingers and threw it out of the restaurant. Sipping my coffee and watching in amusement, the antenna of my mind picked up a few thoughts and started wondering, was the cockroach responsible for their histrionic behaviour? If so, then why was the waiter not disturbed? He handled it near to perfection, without any chaos. It is not the cockroach, but the inability of those people to handle the disturbance caused by the cockroach, that disturbed the ladies. I realized that, it is not the shouting of my father or my boss or my wife that disturbs me, but it's my inability to handle the disturbances caused by their shouting that disturbs me. It's not the traffic jams on the road that disturbs me, but my inability to handle the disturbance caused by the traffic jam that disturbs me. More than the problem, it's my reaction to the problem that creates chaos in my life. Lessons learnt from the story: I understood, I should not react in life. I should always respond. The women reacted, whereas the waiter responded. Reactions are always instinctive whereas responses are always well thought out."

This story, told by Google CEO Sundar Pichai, is a great story. Reading it, the line "More than the problem, it's my reaction to the problem that creates chaos in my life", I was struck by the reality of this for our context — South Africa today. As a leader, I can look at the ugly thing that is racism and react by screaming at it, by jumping up and down or by running away. I am faced with a choice as to whether I will let fear take hold or anger burst forth. I can choose how I respond to the evil that racism and racial tension causes. The cockroach was not supposed to be in the room — it was a restaurant where health and hygiene are of utmost importance. Racism should similarly not exist in South Africa today — we have been a democracy for 20 years already. However, the cockroach is in the room. This book is a story about how we should respond.

The cockroach story is also powerful as it helps us to see the reality and the deeper meaning behind the story. Stories have the power for us to see below the surface — to dig deeper and to truly understand. In a world where time is of the essence, we need to make a decision to pause and listen to the story. In our South African context, our responses to racism and racial issues are a result of our different stories. If we can truly start to understand each other's stories, then we can together start to write a new one.

STORY AS A TOOL

Stories are powerful as they connect us to others. Someone once said that, "stories are state-of-the-heart technology". They create emotional connections that connect our hearts to one another. In South Africa, where so much history, so much injustice and so much pain allowed walls to be built between people, we need to reconnect on a heart level. The laws that defined Apartheid changed 20 years ago, but we still have racism, anger, fear and hatred, because we did not properly deal with heart issues. Jesus, in Luke 6:45 said the following, "The good person out of the treasure of his heart produces good, and the evil person out of his evil treasure produces evil, for out of the abundance of the heart his mouth speaks." My heart's desire is that through these stories we will be able to conquer fear and that our hearts will expand; that we will truly realise that we are better together.

STORIES ALLOW US TO SEE OUR COMMON HUMANITY

As we share our stories, as we peel back the layers of our lives with each other, we get to see the person behind the action. We hear the hurt behind the feeling. We see that the person sharing the story is much like us. As we unpack the feelings and emotions associated with a story, we get to understand why things are as they are. We go beyond the theoretical to the actual. One of the stories you will hear later in the book is that of Thobi Shange. Thobi grew up as the daughter of a housekeeper for a white family. She was treated like a servant in the house, rather than a daughter. She grew up on her mom's employer's property, but shared one room with her mom which was their kitchen, dining room and bedroom. She was told that she would never amount to much because of where she came from. Her future was mapped out for her because she was black, a woman and the daughter of a domestic worker. As one listens to this story and as one gets to know Thobi, you can hear the pain in her voice as she tells this story, but you can also hear her resilience in throwing off these labels to become who God has called her to be. As we hear Thobi's story, we connect with her humanity. Hearing her story, we can understand some of her feelings towards white people. In a similar way, this book allows us to understand others telling their stories.

STORIES SHAPE OUR IDENTITY

Our identity is shaped as we go through life by our upbringing, by our experiences and by the stories we are told and the stories we live. Stories shape our identity for good or bad depending on which stories we are listening to. For example, if my grandfather had a bad experience with a Jewish businessman, I might get told continuously to avoid Jewish businessmen. The story around this businessman frames my view of other Jews as I encounter them. In a similar way, many South Africans have been told stories about those of other races. Black parents have warned their children about the dangers of white people. White parents have warned their children about the dangers of black people. Our interaction with people of other races, languages or religions is framed by these stories and we then respond to these people on the basis of the stories we have been told. However, once we get to know the person behind the story, then all of the protective layers start to fall away and we get to see the real person. Only then can we see the true, authentic identity of the person facing us.

At our church we recently held a workshop series called *What's Your Story?* People of different races and backgrounds sat around small tables and shared their stories. During this powerful experience, I noted something interesting. We are even prone to create our own stories through our internal dialogue. For example, during the session, a young lawyer stood up and shared how she goes through her working week wondering whether she got the client she did based on the fact that she is a very capable lawyer or based on the fact that she is black. A white businessman then shared how his internal dialogue kept asking whether he was not progressing through the company he worked for because he was white. We all have internal dialogues that frame how we view and how we react to the world. It is only as we are truthful about these stories that we can start to understand one another and move forward.

WHAT MAKES A GOOD STORY?

We all love a good story. These are the stories we tell over and over again. Stories come in many forms but Carmine Gallo, in her book *The Storytellers Secret*[3] reflects that a good story has a challenge (some significant problem that needs to be overcome), a struggle (a battle that needs to be won, something that the hero needs to overcome) and a resolution (a description of how the story ends — how the battle was won).

For example, think of the story of South Africa in 1994. We had the significant challenge of Apartheid to overcome. Apartheid had created a story for generations — defining people and their lives and futures by the colour of their skin. Apartheid had created incredible pain, hurt and loss in the lives of millions. It was an evil system that looked too entrenched to overcome. However, people from across the political spectrum rose up against this challenge. The struggle against Apartheid continued over decades. The armed struggle of the ANC led by Nelson Mandela started to challenge this system of inequality and racism. People from across the world stood against Apartheid and countries imposed sanctions against South Africa to try to bring the change needed. As a result of incredible sacrifice, deep dedication to the fight against Apartheid and because of God's hand, we slowly started to see the resolution of this problem as Apartheid started to be dismantled. The freeing of Nelson Mandela in 1990 was a crucial part of this resolution, which culminated in the first free and fair elections of 27 April 1994 and election of the first democratically elected government of South Africa.

Standing in South Africa today, we again have the key elements of a story laid out before us. We have a significant challenge — we are more than 20 years into democracy, but our society is still full of inequality and racism. Racial conflict and racial innuendos make the news at every turn. These racial issues are simmering beneath the surface of our nation. In reality, although the laws of Apartheid have been removed, the heart has not changed. The stories we are telling ourselves about those who are different to us remain the same. Our struggle is against the fears and anxieties of white people, the anger and frustration of black people who still see so much inequality, the pressures on coloured and Indian people to fit into this world and the layers of tension that result. The resolution of this struggle is up to us. The end of this story is in our hands as we seek God's face and as we work together to create a better South Africa. 2 Chronicles 7:14 says the following, "If my people who are called by my name humble themselves, and pray and seek my face and turn from their wicked ways, then I will hear from heaven and will forgive their sin and heal their hand." We have hope but to finish strong in this nation, we need to humble ourselves, pray, seek God's face and turn from our wicked ways. God then promises to heal our land.

The central premise and message of this book is that part of this humbling, part of this turning from our sinful ways, part of this seeking God's face is to see those around us as God sees them. We are all created in the very image of God. We all reflect His image. If you look at the problems facing us today, we need to ask the question "Are we better together?" Is this possible? This book explores this question. It unpacks the stories of others and shows how we can be better together.

Photo credit: Talitha Neville

CHAPTER THREE

THE OTHER SIDE OF THE RAILWAY TRACK

SIMON LEREFOLO

➤→

"I learned that courage was not the absence of fear, but the triumph over it. The brave man is not he who does not feel afraid, but he who conquers that fear."

Nelson Mandela

Potchefstroom, my birth town, has a very interesting history. It is known to be a town where Apartheid was birthed. I was born in May 1975, at the height of Apartheid. My dad worked as a cleaner at the fire department and my mom worked as a domestic worker for a white family in one of the white suburbs. The state of our nation played a role from my very origins, as my parents met when my dad helped my mom get her passbook — a form of identity document for black South Africans that allowed them to work and go to town.

One thing that did not make sense to me growing up was that there was a divide between where Whites, Blacks, Indians and Coloureds lived. We used to go to town (where white people lived) about once a month when my mom and dad were paid, to buy groceries. The township where we lived was called Ikageng, which means "build yourself" in the Setswana language. It was sectioned into Black Africans, Coloureds and Indians, with Black Africans living in the least attractive section of the township.

Most people moved from the villages or from land taken by the government to townships, where they lived in two-roomed homes with a toilet outside the house. My home was a two-roomed house, one bedroom and a kitchen, which was my bedroom at night. When my sister was born, my mom and dad extended the house by building a shack (tin-house), which was to be the kitchen and so affording us to have a bedroom as kids. Townships did not have access to electricity then, so it was normal to wake up early in the morning to make a fire on a cast iron stove and heat up the water before getting ready for work and school. Families who did not have such stoves had to make a fire outside and heat up the water and cook outside the house, even in the freezing temperatures of below zero in winter.

THE GREAT DIVIDE

School days were fun times. I enjoyed going to school, except for the corporal punishment that was used at the time. The degree of punishment varied depending on the offense committed, which included getting low grades, late arrival, making noise in class, and so forth. There were times when I had to fund my school fees and school trips, amongst other things, by selling sweets at school, as my parents could not make ends meet. I also had to take up a Saturday job as a gardener to supplement the sweet business. One of the things I did with my first payment as a gardener was to pay for a school trip to the Johannesburg Zoo, but I sadly missed the bus because I was trying to get some food to take on the trip.

The most challenging thing about working as a gardener in the suburbs for white people was the humiliation of not being allowed to go into the house because I was black and that I had to eat and drink out of a designated tin cup and plate that stayed outside the house. These type of things made me feel inferior to white people and reiterated the great divide that existed between black and white people. I was battling with the contrast of the reality that I was presented with. The white part of town was clean, big houses and beautiful gardens. The schools were well maintained with good play grounds, yet a stone's throw away from there, separated by a railway track was a totally different scenario.

Even then, at the age of 10, it was very clear to me that the scales were unequal. I started feeling that it would actually be much nicer to be white than black. I asked myself, "Why didn't God make me white?" and wished I was white because of how much better I would be treated and the opportunities that would open up to me.

THE WHITE PART OF TOWN WAS CLEAN, BIG HOUSES AND BEAUTIFUL GARDENS. THE SCHOOLS WERE WELL MAINTAINED WITH GOOD PLAY GROUNDS, YET A STONE'S THROW AWAY FROM THERE, SEPARATED BY A RAILWAY LINE WAS A TOTALLY DIFFERENT SCENARIO.

Sometimes when walking back from town to our township, white kids would throw empty cooldrink cans at me and call me derogatory names. I ignored them and didn't retaliate, as I was told over and over again by my parents not to respond or do anything if white people attacked me. This, however, caused a lot of anger and confusion in me.

JOINING THE PROTESTS

It was in the early 80s when the students in my township started protesting against the Apartheid government. I remember high school students disrupting classes by throwing stones at other schools early in the morning. We would hide under the desks until it got quiet or we would be rushed out of school, as it was dangerous to stay with that kind of violence taking place. There were some casualties where kids and teachers were injured in all the commotion. This continued for most of the 80s. There was a group of students from different schools that would mobilise to destabilise the Government and make the nation ungovernable. This group later joined the United Democratic Front (UDF).

When I went to high school, I joined the UDF and got involved with the protests. Protests involved not buying food from white-owned stores, destroying government property and not letting government vehicles into the townships.

THE UNITED DEMOCRATIC FRONT (UDF)

The United Democratic Front (UDF) was one of the most important anti-Apartheid organisations of the 1980s. The non-racial coalition of about 400 civic, church, student, workers and other organisations (national, regional and local) was formed in 1983. The aim was initially to fight the new Tricameral Parliament, which was instituted in 1984 with the election of PW Botha of the National Party. Its slogan, "UDF Unites, Apartheid Divides" reflected the Front's broad support of about 3 million members.[4]

WHEN I WENT TO HIGH SCHOOL, I JOINED THE UDF AND STARTED GETTING INVOLVED WITH THE PROTESTS. PROTESTS INVOLVED NOT BUYING FOOD FROM WHITE-OWNED STORES, DESTROYING GOVERNMENT PROPERTY AND NOT LETTING GOVERNMENT VEHICLES INTO THE TOWNSHIPS.

My parents soon realised that I was either going to be arrested or killed. They decided to move me to a boarding school in Itsoseng (which means "get yourself up" in Setswana) in Bophuthatswana. This was a homeland country or puppet state that was formed by the Apartheid government for Setswana speaking people under the leadership of President Mangope. I went to boarding school in 1991, the year after Nelson Mandela was released from prison.

While at boarding school I started to mobilise pupils at my school to support the fight against Apartheid and homeland rule. President Mangope sent an army to our school and it was not a pleasant sight to say the least. I thought I was going to die that day. The movement died very quickly. I was very confused at the time as on the one hand, I had all these emotions against white people, yet on the other, my mom's employers were paying for my boarding school and I could see that they meant good by doing so.

AND THEN GOD CAME IN

A few months later, I joined Youth for Christ (YFC) and was appointed to be on the committee. The committee was funded by the school to attend the YFC Easter Regional Camp in Mafikeng, the capital city of Bophuthatswana. The first night at the camp, the camp director preached from Psalm 139, talking about the fact that the Lord knows everything about you, even when you try to hide, He knows where to find you. That sermon spoke to me. I was exposed to Christianity because I grew up Catholic, and also my mom's employers were believers and had encouraged my mom to visit the Baptist church in our township. This was the first time that I felt like God cared about me personally and there was a reason why He had created me

AT THE END OF THE TEACHING, I COMMITTED MY LIFE TO LIVING FOR GOD AND TO SERVING HIM FOREVER. IT WAS AS IF SOMETHING WAS LIFTED OFF MY SHOULDERS, EVEN THOUGH IT WAS JUST THE BEGINNING OF THE JOURNEY.

black. The words from that Psalm, saying that God had created my inmost being, that He knit me together in my mother's womb, touched me. At the end of the teaching, I committed my life to living for God and to serving Him forever. It was as if something was lifted off my shoulders, even though it was just the beginning of the journey.

A CULTURE SHOCK

I completed my high school education in 1993, the year before the first democratic elections in South Africa. I had received a scholarship to study Mechanical Engineering at the University of the Witwatersrand (Wits). I had transport organised to take me from Potch to Johannesburg on a Sunday morning to get ready for orientation week. The transport we arranged did not show up, so my mom and I had to take a mini-bus taxi with all my luggage to Johannesburg. We walked from Park Train Station to Wits with suitcases and all other necessities I needed for a new life as a university student.

Wits University was more progressive than most other South African universities at the time. It was a melting pot of cultures with different racial groups coming together and living together. To me this was a serious culture shock, to have Whites, Blacks, Indian, Coloureds and other nationalities living together in one residential place as neighbours. Going to the dining hall was an experience in itself.

Ashley Burston who stayed in the same residence (Men's Res) as me invited me to His People Christian Church. I was also a member of a Christian movement called Christian Action Fellowship (CAF), which was predominantly black and I was comfortable with that. I visited His People a couple of times and felt that there was definitely something that was speaking to my heart through their messages — I can only describe it as a sense of destiny, purpose and discipleship. I found myself in a difficult place having to decide which society to belong to, so I decided to go to His People in the mornings and CAF in the evenings. Wits still had a separate black SRC (Student Representative Council) and a white SRC. So there were black student organisations and similarly other movements that only accommodated different cultural groups. The legacy of Apartheid was still very visible. In 1995, Wits University had its first integrated SRC, which was a big shift. Even the SRC President was black. I had the privilege of being elected onto the second integrated SRC at Wits.

MEETING MY BROTHER FROM ANOTHER MOTHER

At that time, His People Church was predominantly white with a few people from other races. The church was led by American pastors, Bill and Connie Bennot. It was at this point that I met Roger and Nicola Pearce.

Roger was very much in touch with Campus Ministry. When I was appointed vice-chairperson of the His People student's society, Roger prayed for the team and continued to support us. There was a great relationship between that generation of leaders and the generations that went before them. Roger had been a leader for the Wits campus ministry society in the former years. There was a bond that developed as we started working together and doing life together as people from different backgrounds. It became evident that we had believed a lie about each other for many years. Rev. Shodankeh Johnson once said, "Proximity brings clarity". By being close to one another, working together, facing challenges together, this statement became very true for us. We were better together.

REV. SHODANKEH JOHNSON ONCE SAID, "PROXIMITY BRINGS CLARITY". BY BEING CLOSE TO ONE ANOTHER, WORKING TOGETHER, FACING CHALLENGES TOGETHER, THIS STATEMENT BECAME VERY TRUE FOR US. WE WERE BETTER TOGETHER.

FIRST ATTEMPTS TO BRIDGE THE DIVIDE

Soon afterwards, I pioneered a Cross-Cultural Workshop with Mark and Nelree Steenhof. The workshop covered the roots of racism, inferiority and superiority complexes, healing and repentance. This was a great opportunity and platform for us to deal with the pain, the fear and atrocities of the past. To say that Apartheid affected all sides of the fence is an understatement.

I developed lifelong relationships and friendships with some of the people who attended the course. One of the guys who became my close friend is Herman 'Monty' Heukelman. Herman happened to come from my hometown, Potchefstroom. He was also studying mechanical engineering and stayed in the same residence as me. We did not meet in Potch, we did not meet at the School of Mechanical Engineering, we did not meet at res, we met at church. Herman and I had one dilemma, when we visited home for the holidays, he would go to Potch town and I would go to Ikageng. We had a huge mountain to overcome. How do we continue to build the friendship we started, in a racially segregated and hostile town like ours?

> HERMAN AND I HAD ONE DILEMMA, WHEN WE VISITED HOME FOR THE HOLIDAYS, HE WOULD GO TO POTCH TOWN AND I WOULD GO TO IKAGENG. WE HAD A HUGE MOUNTAIN TO OVERCOME. HOW DO WE CONTINUE TO BUILD THE FRIENDSHIP WE STARTED IN A RACIALLY SEGREGATED AND HOSTILE TOWN LIKE OURS?

He had to overcome his fear of visiting the township with all that was told to him about black people wanting to kill white people; and I was afraid that Herman's parents would not let me into their house, as was my experience working as a gardener. We both took the risk! We started by meeting at the border between Ikageng township and Potch town and praying together for our town and nation. We saw the fruit of this prayer in the years to follow.

DEFINING MOMENTS

I met my beautiful wife, Lindi, at a 'Youth for Christ' camp and we got married in 2000. At our wedding in Mafikeng (Lindi's home town), we had Coloureds, Indians, Blacks, Whites, Kenyans, Ghanaians, Nigerians and many more people attending. I remember Roger speaking with a translator, translating to Setswana. It felt like we were beginning to see the rainbow nation. My grandmother could not fathom that we had mokgoa (white people) at our wedding.

One of the defining moments of my journey was when I become a pastor at His People Church and Pastor Willem Nel, our pastor at the His People Church in Potch invited me to come and share the Word. At that point I said to my wife Lindi, "Babes, I don't know what is going to happen, let me rather go alone this time". I looked at the address of where the church was; and it was in the same suburb, in fact the same street, where I worked as a gardener. I was sobbing and praying along the way. All the memories of growing up in Potch started coming back. I never dreamt that I would stand in front of white people and teach them the Word of God. When I stood up in front of the congregation, I told them that God works in amazing ways: I left Potch as a garden boy and now I was back as a preacher of the Gospel to the same people that threw tin cans at me.

Photo credit: Talitha Neville

/ABOUT

Simon and Lindi Lerefolo have one son, Lemo and two daughters, Zinzi and Rori. Simon is the Executive Pastor at Every Nation Rosebank and serves on the Every Nation Southern Africa Apostolic Team. Simon studied Mechanical Engineering and Economics at Wits University and worked as an engineer, manager and consultant. Simon and Lindi are passionate about healthy marriages and families, nation building and how governments can be transformed to better serve the people

---

"THE SPIRIT OF THE LORD IS UPON ME, BECAUSE HE HAS ANOINTED ME TO PROCLAIM GOOD NEWS TO THE POOR. HE HAS SENT ME TO PROCLAIM LIBERTY TO THE CAPTIVES AND RECOVERING OF SIGHT TO THE BLIND, TO SET AT LIBERTY THOSE WHO ARE OPPRESSED, TO PROCLAIM THE YEAR OF THE LORD'S FAVOUR."

LUKE 4:18-19

JOURNAL POINTS

1. What were the main learning points for you in this chapter?

2. What was one of the most difficult things for you as a person growing up? (For me it was the fact that I did not want to be black.)

3. What is the railway line you have to cross? (I had believed lies about people of other cultures and my paradigm shifted when I got close.)

4. How can we help those who are still angry or hurt, with the past or the present state of affairs? (Pray for them and invite them to discussion groups.) Do you have any other ideas?

5. How do we as Christians understand "restitution" according to the Bible?

CHAPTER FOUR

IN THE STRUGGLE

DERRICK & PRISCILLA MOODLEY

➤——→

"I have a dream that my four little children will one day live in a nation where they will not be judged by the colour of their skin but by the content of their character."

Martin Luther King Jnr

A MAN ON A MISSION — DERRICK'S STORY

Growing up in an "Indian township" north of Durban was an interesting experience. Going to a mono-cultural school and living in a mono-cultural community restricted our true South African lifestyles.

As a teenager, I was very aware of the need to fight for the under-privileged and poor in our community. I had a standard school experience until Grade 10 (then Standard 8), when the House of Delegates (the government department that was responsible for Indian affairs at the time) was ordered to start charging students a fee for every exam paper we wrote in Matric (Grade 12). Many couldn't afford to pay the fees. I knew then that I needed to get involved and do something about the injustice faced by my fellow students. I co-ordinated a few students to start a peaceful boycott, in an attempt to force the Department of Education to reverse their decision and to negotiate a solution. The boycott included all grades in our school and in the week to follow, spread to all the schools in our community. During the second week it reached other "Indian areas".

> I REMEMBER AS A YOUNG BOY SEEING THE LETTERS "ANC" SPRAY-PAINTED ON A BRIDGE WHILE WALKING WITH MY DAD. I ASKED HIM WHAT THE ANC WAS, ONLY TO BE TOLD NOT TO MENTION THE ANC AGAIN OR WE WILL END UP IN JAIL.

THE AFRICAN NATIONAL CONGRESS (ANC)

The African National Congress (ANC) was formed in 1912 to unite the African people and spearhead the struggle for fundamental political, social and economic change. Their key objective has been to see the liberation of African people in particular, and black people in general from political and economic bondage. Led by Nelson Mandela, the ANC led the struggle against Apartheid and has been the ruling party in South Africa since the first democratic elections in 1994. During the Apartheid-era, Umkhonto we Sizwe (Spear of the Nation) was the armed wing of the ANC, with Nelson Mandela as its Commander-in-Chief. Its strategy was to sabotage targets of economic and political importance, such as post offices, telephone booths, pass offices and electricity pylons.[5]

This forced the hand of the Department to rethink their decision, which was subsequently reversed. This marked the beginning of my political walk.

I became increasingly aware of the injustice faced by the majority of the people in our country. The acting principal of our school found out about my involvement in the boycott and we started meeting during lunch breaks to discuss the political situation in the country and the sacrifices that needed to be made to see the people of South Africa truly free.

I remember as a young boy seeing the letters ANC spray-painted on a bridge while walking with my dad. I asked him what the ANC was, only to be told not to mention the ANC again or we will end up in jail. I never understood what that meant, but did not mention it again to him. It was only during my discussions with the principal that I realised how serious this was.

JOINING UMKHONTO WE SIZWE

At the age of 15 I had my first Apartheid era encounter with a white person. On a day outing with school friends I desperately needed to use the bathroom while walking back to Durban central. I ducked into a pub and asked the guy at the counter if I could use the bathroom. He got very angry. Surprisingly, he wasn't angry because an under-aged youngster walked into a pub, it was because an "Indian" person walked into a whites-only pub. He responded by pushing a shot gun into my face and screamed the word Koolie. Using some very colourful words, he told me to leave the pub.

This further enraged me and pushed me to get involved in the anti-Apartheid efforts. I joined the underground movement through the African National Congress (ANC). I did some basic MK (Umkhonto We Sizwe) training. MK was the armed wing of the ANC. I was recruited to be shipped out to Russia for further training at the end of Standard 9 (Grade 11), but decided to complete my schooling before leaving South Africa. At the end of my Matric year all major training operations were put on hold and we were asked to stand down. The following February, the news came of Comrade Nelson Mandela's release and the unbanning of all liberation movements. Our order then made sense.

DISCOVERING MY FAMILY'S INVOLVEMENT IN THE STRUGGLE

After I started working with the ANC, I became aware of my family's involvement in the liberation movement. My grandfather was a member of the South African Communist Party in the 1960s. Our family home was used as a base for high-level meetings and co-ordinating the liberation movement operations. My grandparents' home was continuously raided by the Special Branch Police. I recall my grandfather telling me that he made the decision to leave politics behind on the day that my aunt, who was two years old at the time, was thrown into the back of a police van, held by her hair. My grandfather was arrested and he served a nine-month prison sentence for occupying a "white-only" park as part of the passive resistance movement led by Mahatma Ghandi. My dad was just nine months old at the time.

MEETING COMRADE NELSON MANDELA

I continued my work with the ANC and a local community civic organisation called the Phoenix Working Community. In 1993 and 1994, I focused on my work with the ANC leading up to the first ever democratic elections in South Africa. The elections took place on the 27th of April 1994 and this was one of the most satisfying days in my life. The following year, I was employed by the ANC's local Parliamentary Constituency office in Phoenix. I was allocated to serve MP Ela Ghandi and Minister Mac Maharaj.

"WE FOUGHT FOR A FREE SOUTH AFRICA SO THAT ALL CITIZENS OF THIS COUNTRY CAN LIVE TOGETHER IN PEACE AND HARMONY. I SPENT MANY YEARS IN JAIL SO THAT THE WHITE, BLACK, INDIAN AND COLOURED PEOPLE OF OUR GREAT NATION CAN ENJOY THE BEAUTY OF SOUTH AFRICA TOGETHER."

— NELSON MANDELA

I helped co-ordinate our campaign efforts for the 1996 local government elections. During my time in the ANC I had the privilege of meeting Comrade Nelson Mandela on three different occasions. I had many interactions with many ministers, deputy ministers and leaders of the ANC, some of them who currently serve in high-level positions within the ANC and government.

Some of these experiences left lasting impressions on me and helped shape who I am today. One of these was sitting in a leaders meeting with ANC President Nelson Mandela. He was briefing us on the vision for the ANC just before the transitional government started negotiations leading up to 1994. I remember his words clearly, "We fought for a free South Africa so that all citizens of this country can live together in peace and harmony. I spent many years in jail so that the White, Black, Indian and Coloured people of our great nation can enjoy the beauty of South Africa together." He encouraged us to let hatred go and embrace all cultures so that we can see a truly free South Africa blossom into the country it was meant to be.

A LIFE-CHANGING MOMENT

In June 1996, I experienced a life-changing moment. I had managed to launch the first ANC Youth League branch in Phoenix. I was elected as Secretary and the person elected Treasurer was Priscilla Naidoo. Over the next few months, Priscilla and I became close friends and because of her encouragement and prayer, I gave my heart to Jesus on 4 November 1997.

Back then the church discouraged mixing politics and church life. I made a crucial decision to give up my political career to serve the Lord Jesus — a decision that I now know was a life-saving move. I really appreciated the spiritual guidance from Priscilla and Pastor Brian Dolan. Without the leading and guidance of the Holy Spirit, I know I would have not been able to make this important change.

The second life-changing experience happened a year later, when I married Priscilla, my beautiful wife. We started our life journey together and have never looked back. The Lord has truly been good to me.

PRISCILLA'S STORY

Seth Barnes said that, "God wastes nothing in our lives. He uses the experiences we'd rather forget to prepare us to fulfil our life experience."

I was the firstborn of three children. Two years after I was born, my dad began to drink heavily. He continued to abuse alcohol and my parents' marriage started going downhill. He began to physically and mentally abuse my mother and stopped supporting us financially. Eventually my parents divorced. My mother gave her life to Jesus when I was ten years old. She worked very hard to support us and put us through school. The people from church paid for bread so that we would have lunch for school, and we collected groceries every month from the welfare department.

"GOD WASTES NOTHING IN OUR LIVES. HE USES THE EXPERIENCES WE'D RATHER FORGET TO PREPARE US TO FULFIL OUR LIFE EXPERIENCE" — SETH BARNES

NELSON MANDELA

Nelson Rolihlahla Mandela is generally seen as a beloved figure in the history of South Africa. This wasn't always so. As an anti-Apartheid activist in Apartheid-era South Africa, he was arrested several times and often portrayed as an enemy of the State. Mandela was also a key member of the ANC, which was a banned political party at the time. He was finally sentenced to life imprisonment during the Rivonia Trial (1963-1964). He initially served his prison sentence in Robben Island, but was later moved.

Nelson Mandela was released from prison in 1990, after being imprisoned for 27 years. He was South Africa's first democratically elected President and served in this position between 1994 and 1999. His focus was on reconciliation, rather than retribution. He emphasised the tackling of institutionalised racism and encouraged racial reconciliation. This gained him vast respect, both internationally and nationally. He was awarded the Nobel Peace Prize in 1993, alongside F. W. de Klerk. In South Africa, he is often referred to as Tata (father) or Madiba, which is his isiXhosa clan name. He is widely considered to be the "Father of the Nation".

Although we were very poor and my dad was not with us, we were happy. My mother made sure we went to church and served Jesus. My pastor and his family lived two doors away and I felt like I was growing up at the feet of Jesus. Pastors Brian and Sandra were brave people who taught me to be all God created me to be. On numerous occasions my dad smashed all the windows of our house, broke into the house and beat my mother up. My mother would run out of the house, taking me with her. She never left me there and we spent many nights sleeping in the park. One night, Pastor Brian opened his door to us and my dad broke all his windows too. That did not deter Pastor Brian.

My mother was mentored by a few ladies in our church and she quickly realised she did not want my brothers and I to have a legacy of poverty. She had a talent for sewing and joined a successful dressmaker who taught her how to sew beautiful clothes. She eventually started working full-time in a factory. She bought a house and is now retired. My parents never reconciled. My dad lives in a retirement home, is now sober and in contact with my brothers and I. When I finished Matric, Pastor Brian paid for me to attend Bible School.

From an early age, I had promised to never drink alcohol. I knew what it can do and remembered all too well how embarrassed I was of my dad drinking growing up. I never invited friends over to my house, but rather I led a quiet and private life. My solace was reading and I began to develop a love for

South African history. The more I read about Apartheid, the more bitter I became. My history teacher introduced me to the ANC in our area. I started attending meetings and I became involved in the ANC Youth League. I distrusted white people and believed they were all guilty of Apartheid.

OUR LIFE TOGETHER

In 1999, after being married for some time, we decided to move up to Johannesburg from Durban — another life-changing decision. We spent three months looking for a church that would become our home. A friend invited us to His People and within the first five minutes of encountering members of the church, it already started feeling like home to us.

This feeling was solidified when they announced a Racial Reconciliation Workshop happening in two weeks' time. We signed up immediately after the service and I (Priscilla) remember thinking, "Why not, maybe I will get a chance to share my bitterness." Sitting in a small group with Rob Gerhard leading the group, I finally got my chance. He asked us to share how we feel about other races. To the surprise of the group I admitted to being a racist because I hated white people. If Rob was surprised, he didn't show it. His answer blew me away, "Get to know us, we are not all so bad." Over the next few years, Derrick and I took up this challenge and today some of our closest family friends are white.

TO THE SURPRISE OF THE GROUP I ADMITTED TO BEING A RACIST, I HATED WHITE PEOPLE. IF ROB WAS SURPRISED, HE DIDN'T SHOW IT. HIS ANSWER BLEW ME AWAY, "GET TO KNOW US, WE ARE NOT ALL SO BAD." OVER THE NEXT FEW YEARS, DERRICK AND I TOOK UP THIS CHALLENGE AND TODAY SOME OF OUR CLOSEST FAMILY FRIENDS ARE WHITE.

As a family we have chosen to be intentional about how we do life. We do not allow people to be treated differently in our home; we embrace all cultures and are tolerant of other people, even if we don't agree with them. We also chose not to compromise on the biblical principles that we have learnt. We chose to expose our children to multi-cultural environments and we will make sacrifices to ensure that this happens. One such example is that we have selected a fully multi-cultural primary school for our children to attend. It is a little further from home and double the monthly fees than two other schools in our neighbourhood, but it's worth the sacrifice.

Trials and tribulations are not foreign to the Moodleys. Two years after we were married we were told we could not have children. The people we could trust with this news were our multi-cultural family in our cell group. They prayed with us, encouraged us, held our hands and supported us through three miscarriages and many tears. We stood on the promise God gave us through a vision I received on a mountain in Pilansberg Nature Reserve. God came through. We had two miracle babies, De'anna Paige and Samuel Preston. God wasn't done however. We had spoken about adopting and in 2014, God lead us to Baby Haven where we met our beautiful little girl, Phoebe Bree. She is a true blessing to our home. God has blessed us beyond our wildest dreams with three wonderful children.

Over the years we have learnt to trust the Lord in His leading of our family. We have allowed Him to add people into our circle and we have embraced the gifts of a truly multi-cultural South African family. We have chosen to serve and build a multi-cultural church in keeping with the vision that the Lord has for our great nation. We will continue to do so in our lives and our ministry.

Photo credit: Talitha Neville

/ABOUT

Derrick and Priscilla Moodley are pastors at the Every Nation church in Rosebank. They have three beautiful children, De'anna, Preston and Bree. With a B. Com Degree in Business Administration, Derrick is the Operations Manager at the Rosebank church and heads up a ministry helping homeless men. Priscilla oversees the prayer and hosting volunteer ministries and is also the director of Malibongwe, a women's empowerment project. They are both studying theology at Hebron Theological college.

"FOR THIS REASON I BOW MY KNEES BEFORE THE FATHER, FROM WHOM EVERY FAMILY IN HEAVEN AND ON EARTH IS NAMED, THAT ACCORDING TO THE RICHES OF HIS GLORY HE MAY GRANT YOU TO BE STRENGTHENED WITH POWER THROUGH HIS SPIRIT IN YOUR INNER BEING, SO THAT CHRIST MAY DWELL IN YOUR HEARTS THROUGH FAITH—THAT YOU, BEING ROOTED AND GROUNDED IN LOVE, MAY HAVE STRENGTH TO COMPREHEND WITH ALL THE SAINTS WHAT IS THE BREADTH AND LENGTH AND HEIGHT AND DEPTH, AND TO KNOW THE LOVE OF CHRIST THAT SURPASSES KNOWLEDGE, THAT YOU MAY BE FILLED WITH ALL THE FULLNESS OF GOD."

EPHESIANS 3:14-19

JOURNAL POINTS

1. What were the main learning points for you in this chapter?

2. Is your local church a safe place to discuss your experiences with racial tension?

3. What can you do to facilitate conversations that bring racism and racist thinking into the light?

4. How can we best deal with this hurt, in our own lives and in the lives of others?

5. Racism stops with me. Do you agree with this statement and if so, what can I do to make it stop with me?

MANDELA

Photo credit: Talitha Neville

CHAPTER FIVE

APARTHEID'S DEEPER IMPACT

SERGE SOLOMONS

⟫——→

"The lack of human dignity experienced by Africans is a direct result of a policy of white supremacy. White supremacy implies black inferiority. Legislation designed to preserve white supremacy entrenches this notion."

Nelson Mandela at the Rivonia Trial of 20 April 1964

In 1985 my brother and I excitedly arrived in a sunny Durban for a well-deserved beach holiday. Upon arrival, we enjoyed the cool breeze and foam-drenched seawater. About half an hour into our merriment, my dreamy state was rudely interrupted by a police officer who violently waved at us from the shore. At first, I thought it was a friendly gesture, but soon realized that something big was amiss. We were being beckoned back to the shore and started walking toward the policeman, who by now was shouting at us angrily. I can't recollect his exact words, except that we were summoned to come out of the sea. The officer pointed at a board a few meters away with the inscription, "Whites Only". In our excitement and apparent ignorance, we completely missed the sign that prohibited people with our skin colour from using that particular beach. He calmed down after we explained that we were from out of town and that we did not see the sign. Dazed and confused, I followed as our escort exerted the authority of his badge with dramatic effect. It was an embarrassing moment as I vaguely recall some passers-by staring at our humiliating ordeal.

Something inside me broke that day. Before this I was oblivious to the reality of Apartheid, but at that moment I felt the brunt of Apartheid's impact in a real and personal way. I only realised later what a profound impact that moment had on me. It took me years to unpack and uncover the flood of emotions stemming from a sense of national illegitimacy, humiliation, anger, fear, powerlessness and resentment for the apparent wealth, success and privilege enjoyed by a minority. That incident became my reference point of dissatisfaction. As a result, I grew to hate the Apartheid policy and those who enforced its evils.

SOMETHING INSIDE ME BROKE THAT DAY. BEFORE THIS, I WAS OBLIVIOUS TO THE REALITY OF APARTHEID, BUT AT THAT MOMENT I FELT THE BRUNT OF APARTHEID'S IMPACT IN A REAL AND PERSONAL WAY.

However, perhaps the greatest impact that Apartheid had on me is that it confirmed, formed and shaped in me a self-concept or mind-set of inferiority. It awakened a crisis of identity — an identity that I was "second class" and underrated in every way as a Coloured person in South Africa. I developed a mental framework that filtered the world into White and Black, the haves and the have-nots, the suburb and the township, the owner and the worker. I so desperately wanted to be the former, but found myself pulled toward the latter.

A DEEP-SEATED INFERIORITY COMPLEX

In my opinion, more than economic exclusion, political isolation and social prejudice, Apartheid's biggest impact was that of creating an inferiority complex in its victims. I see it all around me in the behaviour of fellow "non-white" South Africans. This inferior self-concept is deep seated and defining and I felt it shape my personal sense of meaning and value. Not even economic empowerment, educational achievements, national transformation and every other external positive development can completely uproot it. Ever present, it consistently influences my individual intrinsic value, social status and success drive (or lack thereof).

On the other hand, it solidified in me a sense of entitlement (someone must pay for my suffering), victim mentality (others are to blame for what is wrong in my world) and a dependency mindset (others are responsible for my welfare). In short, inferiority and its tentacle mind-sets have

> THIS INFERIOR SELF-CONCEPT IS DEEP SEATED AND DEFINING AND I FELT IT SHAPE MY SENSE OF VALUE. NOT EVEN ECONOMIC EMPOWERMENT, ACADEMIC ACHIEVEMENTS, NATIONAL TRANSFORMATION AND EVERY OTHER EXTERNAL POSITIVE DEVELOPMENT CAN COMPLETELY UPROOT IT ... I AM CONVINCED THAT NO EXTERNAL MAN-MADE REMEDY EXISTS FOR THIS FATAL CONDITION AND LEFT UNTREATED, WE INVARIABLY PASS IT ON TO FUTURE GENERATIONS.

devastating effects in our world. It certainly had in mine. The effects are further compounded and even shielded by selfish ambition, personal justification and the avoidance of the pain associated with facing it head on. Inferiority accepts mediocrity, unfinished projects, unreached goals and irresponsibility as a way of life. When caught in mediocrity, one opts for blame shifting instead of personal growth. Where resentment and entitlement are rights, irresponsibility is the daily bread. Such is inferiority, always reaching but never grasping.

In time I grew to understand that I was not alone. The entire human race suffers from some form of an identity crisis, but life goes on and we become seemingly oblivious to its impact. I have become convinced that no external man-made remedy exists for this fatal condition and, left untreated, we invariably pass it on to future generations.

FACING THE HATE AND PAIN

Only when I turned away from the preferences and boxes that our world prescribes and requires, to face the hate and pain I harboured in my heart, did I experience the beginning of transformation that brings the restorative healing I needed. Facing the truth (John 8:32) is like pouring salt on an open wound. It is easier said than done. It stings as it sterilizes the area, priming it for healing to occur.

> FACING THE TRUTH (JOHN 8:32) IS LIKE POURING SALT ON AN OPEN WOUND. IT IS EASIER SAID THAN DONE. IT STINGS AS IT STERILIZES THE AREA, PRIMING IT FOR HEALING TO OCCUR. MY HEALING WAS, AND IS, IN PROGRESS.

My healing was, and is, in progress. It is a case of three steps forward and two steps back, or so it feels. There are no shortcuts. God has used my life journey, education and, ironically, the relationships I had with those I resented, as well as more humiliating and painful experiences to minister restoration into my life. Like a master painter using different colours and textures on the canvas of my heart, He is shaping a redemptive work of art. I am not done yet, but all I know is that every time I choose love in a hate situation, the result is compassion and sincere concern. I am moved to prayer instead of retaliation. I recognize the pain, but I also glimpse the hope.

While Apartheid's impact was deep and profound, more important was the scalpel used to remove the cancer of indifference. I have a new identity — redeemed, restored, renewed — and I am filled with hope for our nation. I have hope that our rainbow nation will be one under God.

I dream that our country will be a place where her diverse ethnic groups, live in harmony, mutual respect and cooperation. I dream of building a nation that will be the envy of, and example to, the world at large. A nation where every sports code recognizes the pedigree of our athletes drawn from the strength of our diversity, moulded in unity of resolve; where our children engaging their global peers are filled with the conviction that they are truly proudly South African. I pray that every person would experience the freedom that is in Jesus. Nkosi sikelela Africa!

Photo credit: Talitha Neville

THE COLOURED PEOPLE OF SOUTH AFRICA

From the onset of white settlement at the Cape in the second part of the 17th Century, an artificial ethnicised Coloured identity was forced onto diverse groups of people. This classification was arbitrary: whichever person or group did not fit into the dominant racial paradigm, was termed Coloured. The Khoikhoi and Khoi San people were the original inhabitants of South Africa. As European settlers encountered them, they were assimilated into the term Coloured. Many Coloured people can trace their ancestry through the Khoikhoi and Khoi San. In addition, the Coloured community grew as European residents mixed with the local inhabitants. Slaves were also brought in from countries such as Malaysia and China, and these groups of people also became termed Coloured.[6]

/ABOUT

Dr Serge and Vivien Solomons are the senior pastors at Every Nation Kerk in Johannesburg. Serge obtained his MBBCh from the University of the Witwatersrand in 1996 and worked in clinical medicine for 10 years. He is passionate about Leadership and People Development and has been involved in Leadership Training and Coaching for the last 8 years. He has an interest in neuropath physiology and its impact on leadership behaviour from a self-actualisation perspective. Amongst other things, Serge is also the Director of Leaders in Transformation, a leadership equipping institute that exists to prepare ethical, spiritual leadership for the marketplace.

"SO JESUS SAID TO THE JEWS WHO HAD BELIEVED HIM, "IF YOU ABIDE IN MY WORD, YOU ARE TRULY MY DISCIPLES, AND YOU WILL KNOW THE TRUTH, AND THE TRUTH WILL SET YOU FREE… SO IF THE SON SETS YOU FREE, YOU WILL BE FREE INDEED."

JOHN 8:31,32,36

JOURNAL POINTS

1. What were the main learning points for you in this chapter?

2. What was Apartheid's deeper impact on your life?

3. What are the signs in your life and in your community that an inner brokenness still prevails?

4. Consider the tension between the deeper impact of Apartheid on your life and your new identity in Christ.

THE FLAM

1

Celebrat

signing of

OF DEMOCRACY

CEMBER 2011

e 15th anniversary of the
outh African Constitution

Photo credit: Talitha Neville

Photo credit: Samantha Jackson Photography

CHAPTER SIX

THE BIRTH OF A RAINBOW NATION FAMILY

GILIAN AND VANESSA DAVIDS

⟫⟶

"Families don't have to match. You don't have to look like someone else to love them."

Leigh Anne Tuohy, played by Sandra Bullock in The Blind Side

Gilian and I started courting in 1992, a very unpopular time for a mixed couple to be together in South Africa. The first time I saw him, was a few years before that, at an inter-youth concert, where a whole lot of youth groups got together for a worship evening. I noticed him from across the church, and was very shocked that I, a white teenager, found him, a coloured guy, attractive. I still remember going home that night and telling my sister that I had seen this good looking guy, but he is COLOURED! I was shaken by that.

HEALING FLOWING OUT OF REPENTANCE AND FORGIVENESS

I was employed as the first secretary and staff member of His People Cape Town in 1990. In 1991, we had a full-time team of young campus ministers on the University of the Western Cape (UWC), and I had become friends with the guy that led the team. He was my first coloured friend ever. While I was working in the church office one day, the team came for their first meeting. I was so shocked when one of them was the guy that I had noticed at the inter-youth event two years earlier. I must admit that I was checking him out, very intrigued. Gilian noticed me watching him, and because of his upbringing and background with fighting in the Struggle, assumed that this white girl was watching to see what he would steal (in all honesty). Of course, we only had that conversation years later.

ONE OF THE SESSIONS ON RACIAL RECONCILIATION REVEALED OUR RACISM, PREJUDICE, INTOLERANCE, IGNORANCE AND OUR SIN… AS WE HUGGED EACH OTHER IN REPENTANCE AND FORGIVENESS, THE LORD WASHED HIS HEALING OVER EACH OF US. IT WAS A DEEP WORK OF THE SPIRIT OF GOD.

Another very significant event that occurred, for both of us separately, was when His People hosted SYMSA (The Symposium for the Biblical Reconstruction of South Africa) in 1992. It was a time of trying to understand what the Bible had to say about how to build a godly nation. It was such a significant conference and shook us all to the core. One of the sessions on Racial Reconciliation revealed our racism, prejudice, intolerance, ignorance and our sin. Gilian, a very racial, resentful young man at the time, had God turn his heart inside out. I was undone and changed forever — we both were. I remember seeing that same group of guys after one of the sessions where we were all crying and sobbing. As we hugged each other in repentance and forgiveness, the Lord washed His healing over each of us. It was a deep work of the Spirit of God.

SEEKING GOD'S WILL

Over the course of the next two years, we all became friendlier with each other and got to know each other well, since the team came into the office for weekly meetings. During the year of 1992, Gilian and I started noticing each other more and seeking each other out more for arbitrary reasons. The other guys amongst the five, especially my one friend, started to notice that there was a bit more of a bond developing between the two of us. We were both in total denial and wouldn't give it any thought, although the feelings were there. It was just not done.

In October 1992, Gilian eventually, for integrity's sake, decided he needed to tell me that he had feelings for me. I was so shocked and terrified, because I felt the same way. The big question was, "What do we do with this?" We decided to slowly get to know each other better, whilst praying for God's direction. We had both purposed to not get involved in a relationship unless it was the person we were going to marry. We made a deadline for the end of the year to have an answer from God.

God in His faithfulness gave us both the exact same answer. Yes, this is your life partner, but the timing is not now. So we spent two years being close friends, getting to know each other, speaking about a lot of things, while we waited on God's timing.

We had many deep and lengthy conversations. Getting to know and understand each other's world, culture and upbringing, was a long and often difficult process. I can remember us visiting my parents one evening, and there was a documentary on TV on Apartheid and the Struggle, and what people had been through. I have never enjoyed documentaries or TV and I was really tired that evening, and while Gilian sat riveted to the TV, I fell asleep (not intentionally). This upset Gilian, because it was such an important part of his history, whereas I had a different point of reference to it and didn't feel the need to watch something that

THROUGH A VERY EMOTIONAL DISCUSSION, I REALISED HOW PAINFUL THIS HISTORY THAT WAS SO VERY REAL TO HIS UPBRINGING, WAS TO GILIAN. MORE THAN THAT, IT WAS VERY IMPORTANT TO HIM THAT I BEGAN TO UNDERSTAND AND EMBRACE IT. I WAS VERY HEARTBROKEN TO HAVE BEEN SO INSENSITIVE, NAÏVE AND IGNORANT.

did not affect me (forgive me, I mean no insensitivity, but that was my ignorance back then). Through a very emotional discussion, I realised how painful this history that was so very real to his upbringing, was to Gilian. More than that, it was very important to him that I began to understand and embrace it. I was very heartbroken to have been so insensitive, naïve and ignorant. We then endeavoured to continue the process of us going much deeper in understanding each other's upbringing and difference in culture.

We had to learn how to understand each other as we often had a different understanding of the same word. So we had to, for almost three years, always ask each other, "What do you mean by that?" This was because we would continually offend each other unknowingly. So we had to say, "Explain that to me so that I understand what you mean." It was a tedious process, but so very necessary. We grew up in different families, different backgrounds and different cultures with different first languages, different family values and traditions. It was a mine field to navigate sometimes.

FAMILY REACTIONS

Our parents had various reactions to our relationship. My mom thought that it was just a phase I was going through. Gilian's parents were at first suspicious of me, questioning me and testing my character, but finally embraced me because of my love and respect for the Lord and for Gilian. My dad wanted nothing to do with it. When I phoned him to tell him about our relationship, to prepare him for our planned engagement, he said he never wanted to hear about it again. It was very hard for me. I am his only child, and always had a very tender relationship with him. I was faced with a choice — please my dad and give up Gilian, or follow my heart and more importantly, God's plan for my life. I wrote my dad a letter explaining this, with many tears, knowing that I risked losing my father. Fortunately, his wife convinced him to at least attend our wedding, which they did. Later, as my dad visited Cape Town and got to know the heart beyond the skin colour barrier, things changed. Gilian and my father became great friends and still are.

STEPPING INTO OUR LIVES TOGETHER

We celebrated and rejoiced during the 1994 elections. It was a big day for us, one we will never forget. We got engaged in June 1994 and married in January 1995. Many people tried to discourage us. The most used arguments were, "How will your children handle this?", "What will they have to deal with at school?" and "What will they look like?"

Whenever we walked in public, we would have people stare at us. We would usually be holding hands, and people did not know how to react. Gilian would purposely look them in the eye and greet them, every time. The people wouldn't know what to do with themselves. We could visibly see the struggle on their faces. In 1999, our first child, Mitchell, was born. Then, when we walked in public, they would look at Gilian, look at me, and then immediately look at the child to see what he looked like. He was such a beautiful, good looking baby. Shock! He looked normal and oh so cute.

WE CELEBRATED AND REJOICED DURING THE 1994 ELECTIONS. IT WAS A BIG DAY FOR US, ONE WE WILL NEVER FORGET. WE GOT ENGAGED IN JUNE 1994 AND MARRIED IN JANUARY 1995. MANY PEOPLE TRIED TO DISCOURAGE US. THE MOST USED ARGUMENTS WERE, "HOW WILL YOUR CHILDREN HANDLE THIS?", "WHAT WILL THEY HAVE TO DEAL WITH AT SCHOOL?" AND "WHAT WILL THEY LOOK LIKE?"

YOUR CULTURE, MY CULTURE, OUR CULTURE

The hour I got home from hospital with Mitchell, Gilian's entire family, and even their in-laws, came to "move in" for the day. I was so shocked as in my culture this was a time for us to be alone and bond with our baby — it was a time to adjust to the big change and have as few visitors as possible, usually only immediate family and for only an hour. Gilian's culture was that the whole family comes over, they make meals, take care of the house, look after the baby and come and bond with the new grandchild/nephew/ cousin. Honestly, it was such a culture shock for me that I took six months to get over it. For my culture, and my introverted personality, it was extremely stressful.

When we had our second child, Janelle, I had to tell Gilian firmly that I could not go through that again. I needed to go home and be quiet, adjust, spend time with just the four of us for a week, until I felt ready for visitors. It was a dilemma for him. He knew how important this was to his family. He also knew that he had to put me and my needs before cultural preferences. He phoned his family, who were already on their way, to tell them not to visit just yet. We knew that they would be offended, but I knew I needed to be in a healthy space as a mom with a new born and two-year-old to adjust to. Who we were and our needs as a family had to supersede culture.

The reason that I mention this example is that we had to learn very early on that culture is not right or wrong. It is just what one is used to — tradition or cultural preferences or habits. Gilian could not say that this is the way we have always done it, so it is right. Neither could I say my culture was right. We had to find our own family culture and our own traditions; and had to decide to do what was right for us and in line with the Word of God.

Family holidays, birthdays, special occasions, Sunday lunch — they were different for each of our families. I had to learn to make curry and he had to learn to eat pasta. We had to create our own traditions and culture as a new family unit. His family was very shocked that when we had our annual leave, we wanted a holiday by ourselves. In their culture, the whole extended family plans their holidays together. There had to be a lot of give and take, compromise on preferences, and finding each other and what was of importance.

A WONDERFUL BOX OF CHOCOLATES

We have three biological children. Mitchell, Janelle and Cole call themselves "Twisters" because of their mix. They each identify with different aspects of our two cultures. This means that in some areas they appreciate the white side of culture that I may bring (such as birthday parties) and in others, they embrace and identify more with the coloured culture (like having a great sense of humour).

We then adopted two black girls who are sisters through Baby and Child Haven from the His People church in Johannesburg. We had planned to adopt only one girl, but God had set us up for His plan and we got two! It was an adjustment for our family to make, not because of the colour as our kids don't see that, but suddenly having two more children, and children who were very different to us.

We are grateful that God chose our family to be the forever family for our precious girls, Sima and Gracelyn (who are now 8 and 6). Our eight-year-old, Sima, is very emotionally intelligent and aware of being adopted and she often thinks of her other mother. We allow her to go there, to grieve and process. They will notice that their nose or hair may be different, but that is all celebrated in our home. Children don't see colour. One of Sima's friends at school came to me on the playground one day, and said that Sima had told her that she was adopted. She did not believe her and wanted proof from me. When I told her that the proof was right in front of her, and explained that I am white and Sima is black, she remarked that she had never noticed that before.

We have four "cultures" in our family: one coloured, one white, three coloured-white twisters and two black. We celebrate our differences and our similarities. Sima loves the fact that she loves to read, just like her mom, and plays the piano like her dad. Gracelyn is excelling in gymnastics, just like her brother, Cole (something only God could have put together and worked out). We look for ways to identify with each other and we celebrate the ways in which we are different. We relate each of us to chocolate. All chocolate is nice and tasty, whether it's white chocolate, brown chocolate, dark chocolate or a mix. We are a mixed box of chocolates and we are so thankful that we can visually display the heart of God through our rainbow family. We count it a privilege that He would find us worthy of this great call.

/ABOUT

Gilian and Vanessa Davids currently lead the city-wide Every Nation churches in Cape Town and pastor the Every Nation West Coast congregation. Gilian started ministry as a campus minister in 1991, whilst Vanessa served as the first staff member of His People Cape Town in 1990. They were both ordained as full-time pastors in 1999. Gilian also serves as a member of the Every Nation ALT (Apostolic Leadership Team) in Southern Africa. He flows in the prophetic and has a passion for worship and serving leaders. Vanessa's passion for ministry centres on seeing people's lives filled, touched, healed and made whole by the supernatural power of God's Spirit working within them. They have been married since 1995 and have five wonderful, rainbow nation children.

"HERE THERE IS NOT GREEK AND JEW, CIRCUMCISED AND UNCIRCUMCISED, BARBARIAN, SCYTHIAN, SLAVE, FREE; BUT CHRIST IS ALL, AND IN ALL. PUT ON THEN, AS GOD'S CHOSEN ONES, HOLY AND BELOVED, COMPASSIONATE HEARTS, KINDNESS, HUMILITY, MEEKNESS, AND PATIENCE, BEARING WITH ONE ANOTHER AND, IF ONE HAS A COMPLAINT AGAINST ANOTHER, FORGIVING EACH OTHER; AS THE LORD HAS FORGIVEN YOU, SO YOU ALSO MUST FORGIVE. AND ABOVE ALL THESE PUT ON LOVE, WHICH BINDS EVERYTHING TOGETHER IN PERFECT HARMONY."

COLOSSIANS 3:12-14

JOURNAL POINTS

1. What were the main learning points for you in this chapter?

2. Consider what you have learnt about the upbringing and customs or traditions of people of different cultures?

3. Have you been in their homes and eaten their food? What can you change in your life in order to do this?

4. Do you have close friends who are of a different race than you, or do you mostly have friends who are the same as your race and your comfort zone? If so, how can you build friendships with other people?

Photo credit: Rochelle Fouché from Hannah Blue

Photo credit: Sherry Neville

COURAGE

CHAPTER SEVEN

CALLED TO BUILD BRIDGES

WILLEM NEL

➤——→

*"I alone cannot change the world, but I can cast a stone
across the waters to create many ripples."*

Mother Theresa

"Then I will give them one heart, and I will put a new spirit within them and take the stony heart out of their flesh, and give them a heart of flesh" Ezekiel 11:19.

I am a living, walking testimony of this truth. The Lord changed my heart of stone into a heart of flesh. He turned my fears into faith and my hate into love. He made me a builder of bridges so that people could cross over to the other side.

RIGHT-WING POLITICS

Growing up, I was very interested in politics. Political events and political news have always fascinated me, so much so that in Grade 8 (then Standard 6) when my teacher asked what I wanted to be when I grow up, I answered, "the President of the country", and I meant it.

I have always believed that I could be instrumental in the process of transformation in our country. Unfortunately, my political aspirations were fueled by fear and not faith. I grew up in Apartheid South Africa as an Afrikaans boy. From my vantage point at the time, I was convinced that I needed to do everything in my power to fight to save our country, to keep it safe, to stay alive and to have a future.

During school, I actively participated in political debates and at university. I became a member of a right-wing group, the AWB, known for their racial hatred and inciting action. Soon I became engulfed in politics. I was involved with the student newspaper, radio station, and was later elected onto the student parliament on campus. I served on the AWB's provincial political structures and was a potential candidate for parliament at one point.

THE AWB

The AWB or Afrikaner Weerstands-beweging (Afrikaner Resistance Movement) is a South African far-right separatist political and para-military organisation, often described as white supremacist group. In its heyday in the 1980s and 1990s, when the nation was moving towards the new democracy, the organisation received much publicity. The AWB was formed in 1973 by Eugène Terre'Blanche who remained the leader until he was murdered on his farm in 2010. Terre'Blanche was succeeded as leader by Steyn van Ronge.[7]

MY PERSONAL TRANSFORMATION

Then God came in. Following an AWB recruitment tour, I went home to visit my parents. They invited me to go to church with them. I decided to go, not knowing that it was a prophetic service. At the end of the service one of the speakers prophesied over my sister and I. I was so afraid in that moment! What if he proclaimed all my sins in front of my parents? What he said, however, touched me in the most profound way. He said that God would remove my heart of stone and replace it with a heart of flesh; that God would give me visions of people in hell and that He has called me to lead people to Him. When we got home I called my girlfriend at the time and asked whether she was going to serve the Lord with me. She got the fright of her life and I think she's probably still running now! It was unthinkable for her that I would resign from my political position. It was only after I met my wonderful wife, Celesté, that the Lord confirmed my calling.

One of my most significant personal transformations came about when I met Pastor Antony Constance of Potchefstroom. The Lord used him to teach me the true meaning of transformation. As a Coloured man, he had a great influence on me becoming a bridge-builder.

TAKING UP THE CALL

In 1992, while I was a chaplain in the National Defense Force and Celesté was a lecturer at a Bible School in Johannesburg, the Lord called us to Potchefstroom. We were reluctant to move. I had a music business in Johannesburg and loved the fast pace of the city. The countryside felt too slow for my taste, but we decided to be obedient and moved soon afterwards.

Potchefstroom is a university town and we started off as chaplains for a campus ministry. We soon realised that all the churches in the town were ministering to white students only. This was the norm, however, as it was before the fall of Apartheid. The Lord gave us a clear Word that He had called us to build bridges between people of all races, generations and even between churches. We knew that we were to minister the Word to everyone we came in contact with, whether black or white, including the staunchly conservative faith community around us.

We faced many problems in the town that God had placed us in. However, God is merciful and He used many people and conferences to prepare us for a time such as this. Some of these problems included:

- Great poverty, especially among the black community.

- Extreme racism, especially from the students who attended the Agricultural College. They would drive around town at night, looking for black people to harass, then beat them with horsewhips (among other things) and the police did nothing to stop them.

- The town was split by politics and religion.

- Economic development was stilted. The town's founders wanted to guard the quality of life they were experiencing and the peace and quiet of the town. This attitude meant, however, that a small minority grew rich and the rest of the community suffered. At one stage, the lecturers at the local university (a significant number of people in the town work for the university) were paid amongst the lowest wages in comparison to other South African universities.

POTCHEFSTROOM HERALD:

IN CONVERSATION WITH PASTOR WILLEM NEL

For a young couple in the ministry, the tranquillity of Potchefstroom is just what the doctor ordered after nine and a half years in Johannesburg. "You can still go for a quiet walk in the evenings here," they said.

The Herald visited Pastor Willem Nel and his wife Celesté. Willem is the pastor of the Potchefstroom Apostolic Faith Mission Student Church. They have been in Potchefstroom now for almost two years. He was also a chaplain in the Defence Force for a year.

Willem says that they started this congregation in 1993 and what makes it unique is that it is the first Pentecostal Charismatic church that ministers exclusively to students. This congregation is under the patronage of the AFS Central Congregation.

The Nels believe they have specifically been called to Potchefstroom to help build bridges between people and church groups. They also focus specifically on addressing the wrongs of the past.

Willem and Celesté are both alumni of the former Rand Afrikaans University and what really struck them about the Potchefstroom students is that they are genuine "peoples-people." Willem and Celesté met each other at RAU during the inter-universities sports day and got married after completing their studies.

Willem is also involved in the National Students' Ministry and has a special interest in computers. Celesté says that her husband likes technology that simplifies one's life.

Celesté is not only actively involved with the students, but is also involved in training people for children's ministry.

The local newspaper published a story on Celesté and I when we arrived in Potchefstroom (see excerpt). To me, this story is evidence that the Lord always fulfills his Word, because He had removed my heart of stone and had given me a heart of flesh — a heart with a passion for people of all races.

FACING OPPOSITION

Looking back, I remember when we first started talking about our desire to bring transformation to our city. This was in the early 1990s, before the birth of the new South Africa. We experienced a great deal of opposition from various sources. One thing that was taboo in Potchefstroom at that time was having multi-cultural church services. My eldest son was dedicated to the Lord in 1995 by my friend, Pastor Anthony Constance. One of our church members, Frieda Kishi, was the first black student to be awarded a leadership position on the university campus. She was also the first black committee member of her university residence management team. As exciting as this was, we felt serious opposition from the management of our church denomination as they tried to remove me as pastor, because of my desire to welcome people of all races into our church services.

One of our student's parents contributed generously to our ministry. One day, the student "called me in" to inform me that her family was going to withdraw their support if I didn't stop this "ministry to blacks". I was able to confidently tell her that neither her, nor her family, took care of me. God had called us and He was our source. For a few months our finances did not look great because her family, as well as others they had influenced, had withdrawn their financial support from our ministry, but we stood firm on the Word of God and as always, God came through.

ONE DAY HE TOOK ME ASIDE AND TOLD ME THAT HE "REALLY WANTED TO BLESS US". HOWEVER, HE HAD A CONDITION – WE HAD TO STOP OUR MULTI-CULTURAL MINISTRY AND ONLY MINISTER TO WHITE STUDENTS. WE DECIDED TO GET BY WITHOUT HIS CONTRIBUTIONS … FAITH IN GOD MEANS THAT YOU STAND FOR WHAT IS RIGHT, NOT FOR WHAT IS COMFORTABLE.

There was another account of a farmer from our region who used to support us financially during the early 1990s. For a young campus preacher, this support was like manna from heaven. One day he took me aside and told me that he "really wanted to bless us". However, he had a condition — we had to stop our multi-cultural ministry and only minister to white students. We decided to get by without his contributions, rather than giving in to his demands, despite this having a significant impact on our pockets. Faith in God means that you stand for what is right, not for what is comfortable in the moment.

Today we lead fully multi-cultural churches in three towns — Potchefstroom, Klerksdorp and Parys. We were able to build our own building and opened His People Faith City Potchefstroom in 2015 (soon to be called Every Nation Faith City). The Lord has showered us with blessing upon blessing over the years. We stand as a living testimony of the Lord's goodness, faithfulness and his love for all — no matter what background, social standing or race. May He be glorified in our nation and may we stand as one.

* Excerpts from Willem Nel's book *Making the Impossible Possible*, as well as his unpublished book *A Bigger World*, were used in this chapter.

/ABOUT

Willem and Celesté Nel are the Lead Pastors of Every Nation Faith City — a multi-cultural, multi-generational and multi-site church based in Potchefstroom, Klerksdorp and Parys, South Africa. They have four beautiful children, Guilliam, Charmoré, Ann-waniq and D'lanrew. Willem serves on the Every Nation Apostolic Leadership Team in Southern Africa.

Willem founded Faith Story Publishing, a publishing house dedicated to making God famous by telling faith stories of ordinary believers who have a passion to share the Good News of the Gospel all over the world. Willem's first book, *A Silent Adventure*, shares his remarkable story of healing and adventure into grace. His second book Making the Impossible Possible was released in February 2015. Willem is a motivational speaker, preacher and executive life coach. His life is marked with a strong word of faith, with healings and miracles a part of his ministry. He lives in Potchefstroom, South Africa and, along with other leaders, is involved with transformation in the region.

JOURNAL POINTS

1.   What were the main learning points for you in this chapter?

2.   Consider the opposition and discouragement that you are facing at the moment. What can you do to overcome these obstacles?

3.   What or who has the ability to discourage you? (If you know this, you will know what the enemy will use to take you from your life's purpose.)

4.   Ask your friends and acquaintances to tell you their life story. Ask questions about their upbringing and their economic and educational background. How do you think this will help in building bridges?

5.   What did you "hear" when they told their story? What would you love to fix or change? (Do not try to fix them, but use this to trust God to give you wisdom and guide your actions.)

Photo credit: AlexanderSmith Photography

Photo credit: Charles Haiyah

CHAPTER EIGHT

STAYING POWER

SIVIWE NOTSHE

➵⟶

"It's not that I'm so smart, it's just that I stay with problems longer."

Albert Einstein

I grew up in a little town called Alice in the Eastern Cape, on the other side of King Williams Town. Although Alice is not a town known by the average South African, it does house the famous University of Fort Hare, which was the intellectual hub for many popular African leaders and politicians such as Archbishop Desmond Tutu, President Kenneth Kaunda, Zimbabwean President Robert Mugabe, Tanzanian President Julius Nyerere and our late President Nelson Mandela, to name a few.

When I was in Standard 1 (Grade 3), I moved from a RDP (Reconstruction and Development Programme) school — where they served us peanut butter sandwiches every day for lunch to the point that you wanted to die whenever you saw the Black Cat peanut butter advert on TV — to a new school called Davidson Primary. Unlike my previous school, this one had interesting extra-curricular activities like drama, painting and even a bit of knitting and sewing (which I never tried, of course).

THE UNIVERSITY OF FORT HARE

The University of Fort Hare is situated in Alice, Siwive's birth town. This university was a key institution of higher education for black Africans from 1916 to 1959. First started as a missionary school, it offered a Western-style academic education to students from across sub-Saharan Africa, creating a black African elite. Fort Hare alumni were part of many subsequent independence movements and governments of newly independent African countries. In 1959, the university was subsumed by the Apartheid system, but it is now part of South Africa's post-Apartheid public higher education system.

Several leading opponents of the Apartheid regime attended Fort Hare, among them Nelson Mandela and Oliver Tambo of the African National Congress, Mangosuthu Buthelezi of the Inkatha Freedom Party, Robert Sobukwe of the Pan Africanist Congress, Desmond Tutu, Kenneth Kaunda, Julius Nyerere, Robert Mugabe and Joshua Nkomo. Nelson Mandela who studied Latin and physics there for almost two years in the 1940s, left the institution as a result of a conflict with a college leader. He later wrote in his autobiography that "For young black South Africans like myself, it was Oxford and Cambridge, Harvard and Yale, all rolled into one."

During the Apartheid years, the school was nationalised and segregated along racial and tribal lines. It became part of the Bantu education system and teaching in African languages rather than English was encouraged. After the end of Apartheid, Oliver Tambo became Chancellor of the University in 1991.[8]

After a year or two in Davidson, a girl named Grace joined our school. She was a white girl with long blonde hair and a high-pitched voice, and she always had a smile on her face. To be honest, it was kind of scary. She was way too happy for a white kid who had just moved into an all-black neighbourhood. Up until this point, I had only viewed white people through the lenses of authority. They were my teachers and headmasters. For the first time, I had to entertain the possibility of a white person being a friend or an equal. I have since envied Grace's joy and poise in her transition. I am by no means claiming that she didn't have her own struggles or levels of discomfort, nor do I claim to know whether or not her joy wasn't a well-fitted mask to cover up her fear.

THE CHOICE AND COMMITMENT TO STAY

What I find to be honourable is the fact that she stayed. Therein, for me, lies the hard work of developing a multi-cultural community — the choice and commitment to stay. To stay connected to those who are different from you, to stay engaged, knowing who people are and where they come from. To stay honest about the challenges facing us as a community and the solutions needed for collective benefit. To stay humble as we recognize our own privilege, pain and responsibility. To stay clear from assumptions and rather seek to know the realities that exist and affect those around us. Lastly, to stay hopeful in God's ability to restore, renew, redeem, reconcile and reform our great nation. The Apostle Paul says it this way in Ephesians 4:2-3, "With all humility and gentleness, with patience, bearing with one another in love, eager to maintain the unity of the Spirit in the bond of peace".

A NEW CONSCIOUSNESS

The memory of Grace resurfaced in my mind almost two decades later, when I was 25. My wife and I, along with our four-month old daughter, packed our bags and moved to Seoul, South Korea, as missionaries. Like Grace, we found ourselves sheepishly smiling in an unfamiliar world. The language was beautiful but hard to grasp. The culture was different but interesting. Seeing another black person was about as common as Bafana Bafana (our national soccer team) winning a soccer game. Seriously though!

It was during this season that what Steve Biko referred to as "consciousness" was awoken in me. The first thing that probed my thinking was observing how differently South African expats related to each other on foreign land. The joy and public affection towards one another, irrespective of race, was something I could only compare to how South Africans treat each other when we accomplish some huge sporting achievement. On foreign ground, we weren't just tolerating each other, but authentically celebrating one another. Our history and progress as South Africans became, in some instances, our testimony to many of the South Koreans who were dealing with their own conflict with North Koreans. We could be frank and honest about our struggles, challenges and opinions without the need to be malicious, offensive and defensive. Lest I sound like this was utter utopia, we definitely had our moments of disagreement, misunderstanding and tension. However, we dealt with those things from a different space and with a different heart.

In this World, but not of this World

Maybe Paul was on to something when he said that we should live as foreigners or aliens, a people who are in this world but not of this world. In other words, we are to be fully in the world for the expression of God's purpose over our lives and the quest of experiencing all of life through the multi-coloured lenses of our Maker. However, we are not of this world because we derive ultimate value, significance and belonging from another world and another source — the Kingdom of God.

THE DOGMA, NARROW PERSPECTIVES AND HARMFUL VALUES IN OUR CULTURE OFTEN TAINT THIS PASSIONATE PURSUIT OF A MEANINGFUL EXISTENCE: THIS IS WHY WE NEED TO BE "NOT OF THIS WORLD". GOD, NOT MAN, DEFINES THE VALUE OF A HUMAN.

I believe this perspective allows us to engage matters of justice, poverty, racism, brokenness, abuse, hatred and other ills of the world passionately and meaningfully. We all need to realize that with the little time we have on earth, we can and must make a difference in the lives of those around us.

The dogma, narrow perspectives and harmful values in our culture often taint this passionate pursuit of a meaningful existence. This is why we need to be "not of this world". God, not man, defines the value of a human. The values and standards of life are defined by the Maker, not His creation.

THE RECONSTRUCTION AND DEVELOPMENT PROGRAMME (RDP)

The Reconstruction and Development Programme (RDP) was instituted post-1994 to address the many social and economic problems facing South Africa. One of the main areas of concern for the RDP was the improvement of living conditions for both rural and urban communities, through projects aimed at improving facets of life such as health care, housing and education. RDP houses are small, low cost houses that have been built in areas that previously lacked proper housing for its inhabitants. Similarly, RDP schools provided very minimal school amenities.

A PREJUDICED WORLD

The second mind-bending experience that lead to my newly found "consciousness" was watching how differently Koreans treated white foreigners compared to black foreigners. After a while of noticing certain people refusing to sit next to me in trains or buses, or people clenching their bags or briefcases when they were around me, and other occurrences that are not worth mentioning, I eventually asked one of my Korean friends to explain why all this was happening. His response was simple and honest, "Growing up," he said, "we were taught to believe that white people were better; better educated, well mannered, better looking." According to him, this way of thinking is the reason for the Korean media constantly presenting a message of 'lighter skin is more beautiful'.

> I DO NOT WANT MY CHILDREN TO FACE THE UNFOUNDED ASSUMPTIONS AND PRE-JUDGEMENTS OF A MISINFORMED AND PREJUDICED WORLD. THIS IS WORTH FIGHTING FOR.

He went on to explain that his understanding of black Africans was that most of them lived with animals; they were primitive, barbaric and athletic and thus were only good in sports or anything that required physical mastery. Of course, it was a shock for him when he realized how bad I was at basketball. There is a narrative that history has created that has taught the world to perceive human value and significance on the basis of one's skin colour and ethnicity. I do not want my kids to face the unfounded assumptions and pre-judgements of a misinformed and prejudiced world. This is worth fighting for.

I miss Korea. I often find myself daydreaming about returning back to give it another shot. I grew to love the people and the culture deeply. My wife and I experienced true affection, respect and love from the many Koreans who we now have the privilege of calling our friends. I thank God that my family and I went there. We are much richer, wiser and thinner as a result.

NOT BLACK ENOUGH, NOT WHITE ENOUGH

Last year our church did a series entitled, "Not black enough, not white enough". The goal was to unify people that were being pulled apart by party politics, violence, protests, racist social outbursts and unresolved systemic and historic issues. The aim was not just to unify the multi-ethnic church community alone, but rather, to unify the church for the sake of a segregated community. Along with salvation, the Gospel gives us three gifts:

1. The gift of value

The Gospel communicates to the world that we are all equally valuable. God's desire and love for us is demonstrated in Christ's sacrifice on the Cross for all of mankind.

2. The gift of family

The Gospel grafts us into a new family. All those who believe become adopted sons and daughters of God the Father.

3. The gift of the Kingdom's resources

The Gospel gives us the means to access the power, ability and perspectives of a new Kingdom. We never need to be hopeless.

As the church, the called-out children of God, we are called to demonstrate and share God's value for every human life, His desire for a diverse yet unified people and His solutions for the problems of the world. This was one of the toughest sermon series I have been a part of, but definitely one of the most rewarding. As I think back on this significant time, I believe that as a community we made two fundamental decisions together:

- **We committed to being a people of a different spirit:** People of a different spirit are people characterised by hope. They see what God can do instead of what man cannot do. They fight against the giants in the land, not against the people of the land. They accept the responsibility to pray and fight, instead of settling for wishful thinking.

- **We are committed to courageously embrace awkwardness:** People willing to embrace awkwardness are hungry for change. They want to see and experience the ways of God's Kingdom permeating all of life. Therefore, they are willing to have uncomfortable conversations with their family, friends and colleagues. They have settled in their hearts that the discomfort and tensions that come with being in a multi-cultural environment are worth it.

I firmly believe that in all the realities that we face as a nation, we have been presented with yet another opportunity to shout from the rooftops and whisper in the corridors that Jesus really is the Way, the Truth and the Life. May these thoughts encourage you to STAY in the journey.

/ABOUT

Siviwe Notshe is married to the lovely Marcia and they have two amazing children, Ovayo and Khuze. Siviwe was born and raised in the Eastern Cape. He has been a part of the His People/Every Nation family for over 11 years and was ordained as one of the pastors at His People Rosebank in 2011. Currently he serves as the Discipleship Pastor for Every Nation Rosebank and leads the 5pm Sunday service. Marcia also serves as a pastor in the church and is a psychologist by profession.

"WITH ALL HUMILITY AND GENTLENESS, WITH PATIENCE, BEARING WITH ONE ANOTHER IN LOVE, EAGER TO MAINTAIN THE UNITY OF THE SPIRIT IN THE BOND OF PEACE."

EPHESIANS 4:2-3

JOURNAL POINTS

1. What were the main learning points for you in this chapter?

2. How does the Gospel affect the way that you view your ethnicity and the ethnicity of others?

3. What are some of the barriers that you tend to encounter when you speak to others about racism or prejudice?

4. What are some of the ways you could exercise and demonstrate mercy when dealing with issues of racism and prejudice in your community?

5. What are some of the ways you could exercise and demonstrate justice when dealing with issues of racism and prejudice in your community?

Photo credit: Star & Harbour Photography

21

BLÄCK
TOOS

CHAPTER NINE

MY JOURNEY TO FORGIVENESS

BONGIWE MKHIZE

➤

*"Darkness cannot drive out darkness; only light can do that.
Hate cannot drive out hate; only love can do that."*

Martin Luther King Jnr

The morning of the 14th of October marked the beginning of a historical event not only for the class of 2015, but for the country as a whole. The #FeesMustFall movement began at the University of the Witwatersrand, but spread throughout all higher learning institutions in no time. It was initially sparked by the proposed fee increment for the year 2016, which was above the inflation rate, regardless of the already persisting financial challenges that students face annually. However, at the core of this protest was the prevailing issue of inequality that South African people have to face daily.

Was the year that marked our democratic State's twenty-first birthday a turning point not only for the student community but for South Africa as a whole? The tough family moment for difficult conversations had arrived. By the sixth day, the protests demanded the creation of space for dialogue. They had captured the attention not only of other higher learning institutions within the country, but the international community at large. It was difficult for most South Africans to wrap their heads around the legitimacy of the protests, but for the most part, the students remained united and disciplined with a clear vision. There was no longer room to hide behind the mere words of the Constitution. This was a test of whether the rights upheld in the Constitution could provide adequate answers to the needs and heart cry of the students. Some of the engagements that took place left question marks regarding the long-term effectiveness of the Truth and Reconciliation process of years ago, which had attempted to provide a platform in order to address some of the injustices that many people had suffered. How then

STEVE BIKO

Steve Biko played a very influential part in the Struggle. As an anti-Apartheid activist in South Africa in the 1960s and 1970s, Biko was considered an enemy of the State. He was a student leader and founded the Black Consciousness Movement, which focussed on a mission to empower the black urban population. Through his writings and slogans, such as "black is beautiful", Biko aimed to combat the common idea among the black population themselves that they were inferior to their white counterparts. Biko famously wrote, "The most potent weapon in the hands of the oppressor is the mind of the oppressed."

Biko was arrested at a police roadblock on 18 August 1977. His interrogation lasted 22 hours and included torture and beatings. While in police custody, Biko suffered a major head injury. He died on the 12th of September, after being transported naked and manacled to another prisoner. The authorities maintained that Biko's death was a result of a hunger strike, despite the obvious bruises and abrasions on his body. Biko's death caused an outcry as it publicised the brutality of the Apartheid government.

do we respond to the exclusions and prejudices that are interwoven into the fabric of our society, which perpetuate discrimination through various avenues?

As I began to think deeply about the situation at hand, I found myself somewhat excited on many levels at the opportunity to start again to address these challenges. Here was an opportunity for the country to dig deep trenches and build a stronger foundation, where each person could play a role in bringing about solutions and correcting the ills of the past. As the days progressed, one of the things that was becoming evident to me was that there seemed to be a disconnect and lack of trust in the current system due to the perpetuated injustices that remain like a scarlet thread in our society. Poverty is constantly staring us in the face, but yet the Bible in Isaiah 1 teaches that, "I the Lord hate injustice" and charges us to look after the orphan and widow. This led me to think about my personal academic story.

MY STORY

My parents worked hard to ensure that my siblings and I could have a promising future. My father being the planner that he was, drew up a will and filed it with his lawyer. He believed so much in education that he made sure we had a secure future when it came to that.

I later enrolled at the University of the Witwatersrand (Wits) and the least of my worries were my study fees as dad had taken care of this aspect of things prior to his untimely death. This was until one morning when I received a letter from Wits stating that I could no longer study with the institution due to outstanding fees. I knew it had to be a mistake. However, I soon learnt that there was no error. The supposed planning had yielded naught and my dreams were squashed before me. The executor of my dad's estate had squandered the assets that we relied upon to ensure a better future for my siblings and I. I couldn't understand how a white professional woman, who ran her own business and already had so much, could steal from a middle class black person. More than that, she was stealing from an unemployed widow and five children. I went through a myriad of emotions. I was so angry. I was angry at white people, I was angry at life and angry at the situation I found myself in.

A BATTLE BETWEEN MY HEART, MIND AND SOUL

This incident brought back the anger I had harboured toward her race for many years. It led me to revisit memories of how I grew up in a world that rejected me purely because I was black. My neighbours often opened the gate so that their dogs could attack my siblings and I. This was my first experience of being in a white suburban area where we were supposed to be "integrated" and it taught us how to stand up for ourselves amidst these unpleasant experiences. The fights would often get physical. This became part of how we lived. We were shown time and time again that being white was "superior".

In pursuing a Bachelor of Social Sciences degree, I came across a man who was a true thought leader of his time and is still arguably very influential and relevant thirty years after he passed on. I had heard of Steve Biko before, but I probably wouldn't have encountered his material were it not for the prescribed readings that I had to read in the first year political science class. My lecturer was a passionate man and although of British descent, he had a deep admiration for Biko. This made me very inquisitive. His passion for the man was contagious and this led me to buy a copy of Steve Biko's book titled, *I write what I like*. I couldn't wait to read it. At this point I was watching a lot of documentaries about Apartheid South Africa and concurrently reading Biko's book.

One night, I was struggling to fall asleep and I picked up Biko's book. This was the first South African political book I had gotten my hands on. A couple of pages into this book, I suddenly felt uncomfortable. I was uncomfortable being in my skin, living in a stunning cottage on the property of a white family.

To give a bit of background, my sister and I had been invited to live there by our dear friends who had become more family than friends, and we adored them. We spent most days with their children and the couple were not merely friends, but mentors and spiritual parents. So here I was finding myself in the middle of a conflicting situation — a battle between my heart, mind and soul. I knew that they were good people whom I had learnt so much from. We treated each other with mutual respect, but Biko's book was legitimately poking away at certain things that made the picture extremely challenging for me to wrap my head around.

THE CONFLICT IN MY HEART HOWEVER PERSISTED. THE MORE DOCUMENTARIES I WATCHED, THE ANGRIER I BECAME AND I BELIEVED THAT THIS ANGER WAS LEGITIMATE. BLACK PEOPLE HAVE SUFFERED MERELY BECAUSE OF A SOCIAL CONSTRUCT AND NOW I FELT THAT I WAS BETRAYING WHO I WAS.

Every day that week, I would come back from university and the kids would come up to my cottage to hang out. They didn't see that I was black and they had no exposure to the prejudices that were, as a result of political influence, deeply buried in some people. The lenses through which they saw the world were very different and the questions they asked were from a sincere place. We would later go into their home and sip hot chocolate in front of the fire, while playing a wooden block game called Jenga.

The conflict in my heart however persisted. The more documentaries I watched, the angrier I became and I sincerely believed that this anger was legitimate. Black people have suffered in this country merely because of a social construct and now I felt that I was betraying who I was.

THROUGH WHICH LENS DO I VIEW THE WORLD?

Steve Biko said, "The most potent weapon in the hands of the oppressor is the mind of the oppressed". This made me pause and think. I began to realize that I was now using one lens through which to view life. Even the people around me, who were genuinely good friends, were also being analysed through that lens, and ran the risk of being painted with the same paintbrush. I constantly prayed, but even prayer in itself was such a challenge at that point. This was mainly because of the historical context through which the Gospel had been brought into our country and how the very same Bible was used as an instrument for racial segregation and oppression. It was still prevalent in our country and I wasn't sure which "side" I was on. My struggle had nothing to do with the family I was living with, but the stronghold that the past was trying to have over my life.

A week earlier, my life was totally okay and now my world was shaken and all that I believed and knew to be true about life was being tested. What I was certain of was that I hated injustice, but I equally knew that I needed to confront these challenges as they were in themselves beginning to oppress me and that would achieve exactly the mind-set that Biko spoke about.

I began to pray and I remember reading Isaiah 61:8, "For I the Lord love justice and I hate robbery and I hate wrongdoing". This Scripture brought some light in the midst of this challenge. I realised that God was against injustice so I had to take His commands seriously, and choose to let go and forgive.

BREAKING OUT OF PRISON

Nelson Mandela said, "As I walked out the door toward the gate that would lead to my freedom, I knew if I didn't leave my bitterness and hatred behind, I'd still be in prison." I then embarked on a journey of forgiveness, which is even more challenging when the other party is not asking for forgiveness. I chose to do it anyway.

> I THEN EMBARKED ON A JOURNEY OF FORGIVENESS, WHICH IS EVEN MORE CHALLENGING WHEN THE OTHER PARTY IS NOT ASKING FOR FORGIVENESS. I CHOSE TO DO IT ANYWAY.

I knew that being angry at the executor of my dad's estate was not only destroying me in the process, but it was holding me back. One of the metaphors used when describing the effects of hatred is that it is like drinking poison and hoping that the other person will die. This journey had many layers to it and it posed a serious conflict inside of me. Not only was she a white South African woman, but she was also a beneficiary of a system, which led us as black people to the situation that we found ourselves in.

It is often so difficult to extend grace when you feel justified in a particular situation, yet Jesus extends grace to us daily for the many mistakes we make. The more I read the Word of God and prayed, the more I gained understanding of the role of forgiveness. As difficult as it was sometimes, I knew that it was no longer about the other party not asking for forgiveness or even perhaps not realizing that it is also what they themselves need in order to live the free life that Christ promises us. I continued to interrogate the feelings that I had and constantly brought them before God in humility; and it was through this process that I realized my passion for justice. This led me to praying for my diverse country and trusting God for true reconciliation. My prayer had changed to that of Isaiah 61.

MY PASSION FOR JUSTICE

The picture of a white girl and black boy with their heads against each other, taken at the University of the Western Cape during the #FeesMustFall campaign, circulated on social media, celebrating the news that the President had decided on a zero fee increment for the year 2016, gave me a glimpse of a South Africa I want to raise my children in. They had joined hands at the beginning of the protest because someone understood that it doesn't have to directly affect you, for you to stand up for what it right.

If we are going to build our country and go on a journey of forgiveness and healing, are we ready to hold hands and together be at the centre of ushering in true reconciliation with all races involved? Or would we rather maintain the status quo of an illusion of a rainbow nation? How do we move to the beat of the next generation in such a way that we deliberately foster an environment that eradicates the notion of "the other"?

/ ABOUT

Bongiwe Mina Mkhize holds a Bachelor of Social Sciences degree from Wits University and is currently completing her final year in LLB. It was her passion for economic development, justice, education and seeing poverty alleviated in South African communities that led her to resign from her role in the Mining sector and pursue this passion. She joined campus ministry where she mentors students, establishes biblical principles in their lives, trains and empowers them not only to apply their faith to personal salvation, but to their vocations to impact society and change the world. She was previously a Mineral Rights Consultant at Umbono Capital where she played a key role in establishing the Corporate Social Investment Department, which invests primarily in education in impoverished communities. She has experience in corporate communications, leadership skills, managing stakeholders, sourcing funding as well as in human resources.

"THEN PETER CAME UP AND SAID TO HIM, 'LORD, HOW OFTEN WILL MY BROTHER SIN AGAINST ME, AND I FORGIVE HIM? AS MANY AS SEVEN TIMES?' JESUS SAID TO HIM, 'I DO NOT SAY TO YOU SEVEN TIMES, BUT SEVENTY-SEVEN TIMES.'"

MATTHEW 18:21-22

JOURNAL POINTS

1. What were the main learning points for you in this chapter?

2. What injustices have you personally experienced or witnessed around you?

3. How have you processed or dealt with them? Are there specific people that you need to forgive? Take a moment to write down their names, and ask God for the strength to forgive them.

CHAPTER TEN

FRIENDSHIP IN THE NEW SOUTH AFRICA

THOBI SHANGE & JESSE SMITH

➤——→

"What draws people to be friends is that they see the same truth. They share it."

C.S. Lewis

This is the story of our individual lives, and the story of our friendship. It is a story of how the Lord's plans are always higher than ours, and that Jesus truly is the bridge that helps us cross the divide.

THOBI'S STORY

I grew up knowing very well that I am a black girl. I lived with my mother and didn't have a positive fatherly figure in my life. My mother was a live-in maid for a white family. Growing up on the family's property, I was subjected to a lot of verbal and emotional abuse, as well as neglect.

I was told on a weekly basis that I would amount to nothing. One day, the grandmother of the house was eating Brazilian nuts and offered me one to taste. I took it, admiring its large unusual shape. My five-year old eyes had never seen one of these before. I ate it and loved it. While chewing on another nut, she smiled weakly at me and said, "Here, have another one. Enjoy these because you will never be able to afford them on a maid's salary." On another occasion, the mother of the house said, "When you come back from school, you must start looking after the baby, because when your mother retires, you'll be looking after my grandchildren". I was six at the time.

From an early age, these were the words that were spoken over me. This was the expectation for my life. I lived in the back room of the house with my mother. The room was tiny and could only fit in a small ¾ sized bed, a kitchen cabinet, wardrobe, TV and a small stove. We cooked, watched TV and slept in this room. It was not until I was twelve that I got some level of privacy after moving into the storage room next door. Even then, my privacy was based on merit. When I was accused of stealing any item, my room was searched without permission. I recall one occasion in my teen years when I was accused of stealing a jacket and the wife of the son of the house came into my room and threw all of my belongings on the floor while screaming curse words at me and telling me how much of a thief I was. By this time, I had already developed a level of hate and fear for any white person — especially a white man. The father of the house was absolutely cold towards me. I leaned towards him because I was a complete daddy's girl before my father left. I was yearning for approval, protection and affirmation from an older male figure. He, in my young mind, was the next best thing. However, I learned that I was to never speak to him unless he spoke to me first. If I tried, I was blatantly ignored.

EXPERIENCING REJECTION AND NEGLECT

I learnt that I was not to have an opinion because when I did, I was told that I was stupid and that my thoughts had no place in society. I also never received any form of embrace, because I was told that black people smelt like urine and that our skin was dirty. I also needed permission to eat anything. I was not, under any circumstances, allowed to take what I wanted without being watched or given it by them. My mom once had to leave me in the care of the family as she had to attend a family event in KwaZulu-Natal. The family denied me food, warmth or even a bath until she returned. She was gone for two days. I recall the sheer pain that my mother expressed through her body language when she saw me after she returned from her trip.

For the longest time and without knowing it, I detested white people, yet envied the power that they held. At school, I was not accepted by the white kids. Unfortunately, I was not accepted by black children either. They labelled me a coconut, because whilst I was black, I didn't speak like other black kids due to growing up in a white suburb.

FOR THE LONGEST TIME AND WITHOUT KNOWING IT, I DETESTED WHITE PEOPLE, YET ENVIED THE POWER THAT THEY HELD. AT SCHOOL, I WAS NOT ACCEPTED BY WHITE KIDS. UNFORTUNATELY, I WAS NOT ACCEPTED BY BLACK CHILDREN EITHER. THEY LABELLED ME AS A COCONUT, BECAUSE WHILST I WAS BLACK, I DIDN'T SPEAK LIKE OTHER BLACK KIDS DUE TO GROWING IN A WHITE SUBURB.

HATING WHO I WAS AND HATING WHO I WAS EXPECTED TO BE

I just didn't fit in anywhere and was often alone. From a very early age, I was not sure who I was supposed to be. At home, I was not at rest when I was in the main house and often retreated to my small room to be alone until I was needed. I recall hating who I was and hating who I was expected to be.

I had no respect for any white person, but sadly I also had no respect for black men. I grew up in Johannesburg, but went to KwaZulu-Natal for school holidays to visit my brothers and sister. In some areas of rural KwaZulu-Natal, men often do as they please to women. I was treated like a sex object from the time I turned 13. I was touched inappropriately and spoken to as though I was expected to not speak back. I was often told that I was of a "higher value as a wife" because I spoke English and I was respectful. I was not respectful, just quiet! I was looked at as an object to be possessed. I recall being forced into a room by one of my uncles who wanted to have intercourse with me. I escaped only because I injured him, but when I told the story, I was told to never speak of it again because of the shame that would be upon the family. I had heard of so many of these types of stories, some severely brutal, that by the age of 16 I did not believe that I could ever be safe or taken care of. I hated black men for taking what they pleased without permission, but I also hated white people for oppressing my very existence.

I started rebelling as a teen and my rebellion was in full swing by the time I was kicked out the house and living on my own at university. I went to Wits and studied Media and International Relations. I did not complete my studies because I ran out of funds. My sister sadly passed away and I needed to find work to support my family. I left university during my third year.

SET FREE AND ON A NEW JOURNEY

I entered the job market and worked for a few companies before settling into a job that I really loved. Everything seemed to be going very well. I had a great job and I was with "the man of my dreams". Yet, after some time, I started to feel a deep discontent in the way I was living life. The things that I thought were satisfying me, weren't sitting so well with me anymore. One day, when my boyfriend and I were joking and laughing together, I felt so content and I thought, "This is amazing. I could do this forever". In a clear audible voice (to my ears only) God said, "Now imagine how amazing it would be if this was with Jesus". It was a familiar voice, because I had heard it a few times before. I decided then and there to pursue God.

A week later, my boyfriend broke up with me, the company I was working for started disintegrating and I found myself unable to pay rent or even eat. I pushed through because I was determined to know God. During this time, I started attending church. At church, I met an amazing white girl called Jesse. We soon became friends. She prayed for me to be baptised in the Holy Spirit a few weeks later. My life had a 360 degree turn around. I was walking with God, experiencing his healing power in my life, and feeling a sense of great hope for the future. A while later, I started working at the church on a full-time basis.

JESSE'S STORY

I was born in Pietermaritzburg in 1992. Before I was able to remember, South Africa had entered into political freedom. My mother was one of those compassionate and real people who lived what they preached and helped everyone she could. I was thus raised with thick skin (having been told many truths that were hard to hear), and an understanding of people that many don't have. I was made aware of the privileges I had from a young age and I knew that others who were less fortunate were not in their position because they were stupid or lazy. I knew that I was privileged and that it was my responsibility to help those who weren't.

As a child, I grew up in a very multi-cultural setting. Before we moved to Johannesburg, we lived in largely Indian and Black area in Pietermaritzburg. I was given a Zulu name, Busisiwe, which means Blessing, and I was taught to greet my Zulu elders correctly. My sisters and I always had friends of different races and I never saw any difference in race. My eldest sister was a member of the Zulu traditional dance team in high school and she was known as that "white girl with no white friends". It seems like I am known as that girl now, which is perfectly fine with me. Quite honestly I was quite lucky to grow up in such a manner, not having to fight very racially skewed mind-sets as an adult.

WHITE PRIVILEGE

That being said, I know I am not without my prejudices. I had to learn the extent of my privilege as an adult. It was really only through my friends patiently walking me through how regularly racial preference occurs that I began to see and understand where they were coming from. I think they were willing to do that with me because they could see I genuinely wanted to understand. I knew it wasn't my place to justify the things of the past and never tried. I did have many moments of justification growing up though. I remember learning about Apartheid in school and feeling like the way the subject was taught just instilled a greater divide between the girls in my class. It's possible this happened, but I was still seeing this in a vacuum, not really aware of how much racism these girls had to fight off each and every day. I remember being told by a fellow student that I needed to go back to Europe. I was

> I WAS GIVEN A ZULU NAME, BUSISIWE, WHICH MEANS BLESSING, AND I WAS TAUGHT TO GREET MY ZULU ELDERS CORRECTLY. MY SISTERS AND I ALWAYS HAD FRIENDS OF DIFFERENT RACES AND I NEVER SAW ANY DIFFERENCE IN RACE.

hurt by this, and confused, not sure what I would do in Europe. But at the same time, I knew that my hurt didn't compare with hers and so I kept quiet. I remember sitting in a conversation where friends were accusing the vice-principal of being racist. She was one of the greatest teachers I knew and I couldn't imagine her showing any favouritism. I figured that these girls were reading racism into a situation. To me, this made their complaints invalid. In hindsight, when someone feels hurt it is never invalid. I just didn't know this at the time.

I am not without my justifications and prejudices, but my greatest privilege isn't that I am white. It is that Jesus is changing my heart and giving me friends who walk me through the process.

THOBI AND JESSE'S FRIENDSHIP

We became friends in 2014. The next year, we both found ourselves in a situation where we needed a new place to stay. We decided to share an apartment and moved in during the month of October 2015. Jesse wasn't around for the first two weeks and I (Thobi) was enjoying the new living arrangement. It felt like she was there, because all her stuff was there, but I didn't realise how different it would feel with her actually being present. When she came back, I began to feel uncomfortable with having a white person in the same space as me. We had been friends for a few months, but I didn't know how much I would have to adjust to having a white person living with me. Unlike when I grew up, where I still had space to be me, my home was now shared with the same kind of person who had previously made me feel insignificant. I couldn't figure out if I was welcome in my own space any more. Did she mind if I cooked? Did I need to make less noise? How was she going to react if I ate something from the fridge? Jesse didn't notice anything weird. She had lived with black people before, and it didn't occur to her that she could cause someone else to feel like this.

IF THERE IS ONE THING I HAVE LEARNT ABOUT PRIVILEGE, IT IS THAT WHITE PEOPLE NEED TO BE AWARE OF IT AND AWARE THAT THEY CARRY THE RESPONSIBILITY TO DECONSTRUCT IT.

Prior to us sharing the apartment, Jesse had been living on her own for some time. She was used to having her own space and own food. Also, they didn't have a lot of money growing up, so she was used to making things stretch. One day, her favourite mayonnaise ran out. I had been introduced to this delicious mayonnaise and I thought it was the best thing ever. I ate a lot of it and before I knew it, it was finished. This upset Jesse and she suggested that we buy and make our own food. I was already feeling guilty for finishing the mayonnaise, so when Jesse brought it up, I immediately thought she was looking at me as if I was a greedy, black person. I felt as though I was back in my old dark and dingy room, where I was sent when I was not welcome in the house. I felt unwelcome in my own home. My own friend seemed disgusted by me. As I got upset about what Jesse thought was a fair suggestion, she immediately became defensive. Things blew up. I headed to my room, crying. Suddenly, I felt God saying to me that I can't be in this space, living in a prison where I close myself off as soon as I am faced with an emotionally difficult situation. He told me I had to dispel the prejudices I had against white people. As hard as it was, I decided to go and talk to Jesse. As it turned out, she had been feeling convicted about being selfish and would rather learn to share than have a wall up in our friendship. I told her about how the situation had made me feel, owning where I had placed my prejudices on her and giving her the chance to step into my space. Jesse felt bad for not recognising what she had communicated and she apologised for making presumptions about me, for being selfish and inconsiderate.

> THROUGH BEING REAL ABOUT HOW OUR EXPERIENCES HAD SHAPED US, AND THROUGH OWNING WHERE WE HELD ONTO HURT AND PREJUDICE, WE WERE ABLE TO OVERCOME WHAT HISTORY HAD DEFINED OUR FRIENDSHIP TO BE. WE WERE ABLE TO CREATE A NEW NARRATIVE FOR OURSELVES.

Through being real about how our experiences had shaped us, and through owning where we held onto hurt and prejudice, we were able to overcome what history had defined our friendship to be. We were able to create a new narrative for ourselves. Our friendship has never been stronger. Instead of being divided by culture, we were able to form a new one in our home.

/ABOUT

Thobekile Shange is a young lady who is proud of her Zulu heritage, but is even more proud to be seen with Jesus. She was radically saved in 2014 after hearing God's voice calling her back home. She has recently started studying through the Every Nation Ministry School and intends to become a Christian Counsellor. She works as an events coordinator for Every Naton Rosebank as a full-time staff member.

Jesse Smith completed her Matric at Parktown Girls High School and began working with His Kids straight afterwards. She completed her BA Ministry Cum Laude through Adonai International Christian University. She is currently studying a BSc in International Relations through London School of Economics. Jesse completed the His People Ministry School in 2014. After working in kids ministry for three years, she moved over to the discipleship ministry and have been there for over two years. Jesse was ordained as a pastor at Every Nation Rosebank in 2015.

"TWO ARE BETTER THAN ONE, BECAUSE THEY HAVE A GOOD REWARD FOR THEIR TOIL. FOR IF THEY FALL, ONE WILL LIFT UP HIS FELLOW. BUT WOE TO HIM WHO IS ALONE WHEN HE FALLS AND HAS NOT ANOTHER TO LIFT HIM UP!"

ECCLESIASTES 4:9-10

JOURNAL POINTS

1. What were the main learning points for you in this chapter?

2. How did you feel when you read how Thobi grew up? What hurts are you carrying from your growing up years?

3. Can you describe your own white or other privilege?

4. If you have been privileged – white or other – what is now your responsibility?

5. What do you think are the main barriers in cross-cultural friendships? How can we overcome them? Think of people in your church, community or workplace that you can make an effort to connect with.

WHERE THERE IS UNITY THERE IS VICTORY

Photo credit: Star & Harbour Photography

CHAPTER ELEVEN

WE ARE THE NEW GENERATION

THANDO PHELLO & SHAUN PEARCE

➤——→

"Let us become the first generation to decide to be the last that sees empty classrooms, lost childhoods, and wasted potentials."

Malala Yousafzai (Youngest-ever Nobel Prize laureate)

This chapter shares the stories of two young South Africans. One who grow up in a Christian home and one who grew up as an orphan in a children's home. They were born in the new South Africa and their worldview is very different from the worldview of those of us who were born and raised in the Apartheid era. These young people have been dealing with the aftermath of Apartheid all their lives. Having been born into this complex society, they have had to find their way through it all. However, the future of our nation relies on them. As the older generation, we need to start running the race beside them, preparing, mentoring and empowering them to run the race set before them. Let us commit to pray for them and lay down our lives to give them a hope and a future in this wonderful nation. I have no doubt that the Lord's hand is on South Africa at this time. In fact, it never left.

THANDO'S STORY

My mom fell pregnant with me when she was 16 and could not look after me, so she abandoned me when I was seven months old. That is how I ended up in a baby home. When I was around five, I was moved to a children's home. I didn't know anything about racism back then, so didn't understand the treatment I received from some of our carers, I just thought there was something wrong with me. One of the house parents used to treat us black kids really badly. When I used to wet my bed, she used to make me bath in water with ice blocks, for some reason or another!

Being a black kid in an Afrikaans children's home wasn't easy. It was hard to get recognition from my peers. I never used to stay in one house very long, because I was a very troubled individual. I moved at least twice a year from house to house, so I never really had a sense of stability. I always went to Afrikaans schools and it was always the same story — you get there, you get called really bad names, you knock someone out — and that was the way you earned respect and love from others. You also had to learn to forgive and let go. When I didn't, I ended up with more enemies than friends.

When I was 16, I received a Facebook message from a lady who asked if she could meet me. It was strange, but I agreed to meet her. When I got home from school one day, there she was, crying and saying that she was my mom. We spoke and I found out some things like why she left me and that my dad had passed away. I knew her for three weeks and then I got a phone call saying she had died.

A TOTAL CHANGE AROUND

I am now 18 years old and in my final year of school. At the beginning of the year, I felt like I couldn't live at the children's home anymore. All my friends had finished school and moved out. All the older boys had been living in a teenage boys' house, but now I had to move into a home with young kids again. The house parents struggled to cope with me, as I struggled to adapt to rules such as study time being in the afternoon, bed time being really early, and so forth. I just wanted to leave. I called some of my friends but they couldn't take me in. I called some of the family I found out I had, but they said that they didn't know me. I was just tired and stressed out and saw no hope. I just had no plan at all. One day, I packed all my stuff and left. I didn't know Jesus back then, but just felt like praying. I said, "God, if you show me that you are real, I will follow you." For some reason, I decided to go back to the children's home. When my social worker saw me, she asked why I was there and not at school. I told her that I was leaving. She asked me to get in the car and that is when she took me to Home-Base. I met up with Uncle Dennis and Aunty Nicky and we chatted a bit. They told me all about Home-Base, that it was a place where orphans and vulnerable youth, can go to stay and get help and support to study further. There were five other guys and two girls living there at that time, and they all were studying at a college or university. Most of them came from children's homes like mine. For the first time in a long time, I felt hope. I felt like God had made a way for me.

I moved into Home-Base around 15 days later. The people were awesome. The first Sunday I was there, I went to church with everyone. I have never experienced a church like that before. People were so happy and were praising God with all their hearts. I was so touched. A few weeks later, I gave my heart to Jesus. I love going to church and I love living at Home-Base. I want nothing more than to grow in my walk with God. It hasn't been easy though. My friends at school have really struggled with the fact that I am a Christian now. They hate the fact that I don't want to party anymore.

It has been worth the uphill battle, because I know that God has a plan for my life. I also believe that it wasn't a coincidence that I grew up in an Afrikaans home and that Afrikaans is my first language. I fully believe Jeremiah 29:11, "For I know the plans I have for you, declares the Lord, plans for welfare and not for evil, to give you a future and a hope." What's more, I have hope for our nation, because although my generation of young people are still in the midst of trying to overcome the after-effects of Apartheid, I have watched the children around me play and interact and seen how free they are in this regard. It's going to take time, but I have hope.

SHAUN'S STORY

Growing up, I had no real difficulty in making friends with people of other races. I think it was primarily because of growing up in a multi-racial church and in a Christian home where there wasn't an emphasis placed on one race being above another.

They say nobody is born racist, which is very true because when you're younger, all you want to do is have somebody to play with. Even though my primary school was about 50% white, I felt quite integrated racially and had a lot of friends who weren't white. My first two best friends were Zulu and Sesotho. Growing up in a multi-cultural environment from a young age has really helped me. Friends at university who came from primarily white schools sometimes struggle with relating to others. One of my friends came to me and said, "Shaun, I've never been friends with a non-white person before". He isn't racist, he just doesn't know how to integrate himself with others.

IT'S NOT ABOUT JUST TOLERATING SOMEONE'S CULTURE. IT IS ABOUT SAYING IT IS IMPORTANT AND UNIQUE AND, ALTHOUGH ITS DIFFERENT TO WHAT I'VE GROWN UP WITH, LET'S CELEBRATE OUR DIFFERENCES.

In high school, things became more complicated as people don't make friends with the simple agenda of playing games. It became important to explore others' cultural differences. My high school, Parktown Boys, was very mixed. We were one of the first schools in South Africa to become multi-racial. I became friends with Mokgeseng (or MG as he is known), who is Sesotho, in Grade 9 or 10. I remember the first time I went to sleep over at his house. It was the first time a white person had slept over. His parents invited me, because it was important to them. We had traditional food that night — pap and tripe (which MG doesn't actually like). There were no knives and forks offered so I ate with my hands, which showed them that I can relate to their culture and respect them enough to do it the way they do it and see the importance in that. It's not about just tolerating someone's culture. It is about saying it is important and unique and, although it's different to what I've grown up with, let's celebrate our differences.

MG was my best friend throughout high school. Coming from an all-boys school you talk about your brothers — your friends who are like your brothers. He has had my back through the worst times I had in Matric. My parents treat him like a son and that has created a space where he feels completely comfortable. He says that our house is a home away from home, which makes me very happy. The first few times that he came he was very quiet and nervous around my parents, that's just how he is and how he's been raised. But now he's himself. When him and I watch a movie at my house, he always falls asleep in front of the TV. Both of us do.

FREE THINKING

University is interesting in that an emphasis is placed on free thinking, but sometimes the thinking is not quite so free. I was walking down the street one day with MG and we bumped into one of his friends. When MG introduced me, his friend asked me, in reference to our friendship, whether or not our relationship was decolonised. I stopped for a moment and asked him if he could explain his question, because I wasn't sure how to answer it and didn't want to answer it wrongly. He refused to explain and simply repeated his question. MG just looked at me and, very kindly, said, "Shaun, I'll let you answer this one." I just thought, "Thanks, buddy".

Decolonisation is the buzzword of a movement that says that South Africa is not really a rainbow nation and that Nelson Mandela failed us as he was too soft on reform. They say that in order to properly decolonise Africa, we must decolonise our thinking. They throw this word around and I feel like it's a very loosely termed word that changes its meaning depending on what they want to achieve, so you can't quite get on top of what the problem is. It's always this vague term and the moment you try to talk to them, you're accused of thinking colonially. It implies that you can never be on the same ground. I replied, "I would say that our relationship is decolonised. MG and I talk about things and we have racial discussions and we're honest with each other." The other guy then asked, "Well then, if there's a protest and MG's there, are you going to go support him?" I realised that what this guy actually wanted to know was whether I cared about the things MG cared about. I do care about my friend on a deep level and am willing to give up my comfort and my time and make time for him in things that matter to him. That struck me as the heart of it and I said, "You know what, if it's important to MG and he wants me to be there and the issue at hand doesn't go against my personal values, I would be there." It has nothing to do with race, which is what he really wanted to know.

STEPPING OUT OF OUR COMFORT ZONES

In varsity, you get exposed to many different ideas and ways of thinking, and people are no longer satisfied with what had happened in 1994. Many students are racially polarised on both ends. It's important to recognise that people are hurting; and there's usually a very valid reason why they are hurting. How do I, as a person who is on the other side to them, show them that not all my kind of people are against them?

We need to show them that not everyone is polarised, that there is actually progress happening. It means having tough conversations with each other and being even more open and honest. At times, it might mean getting screamed at in your face by someone who is really hurting and just wants to vent their anger. Even when you feel attacked and hurt, and don't understand where their response came from, you need to endeavour to go beyond yourself, knowing that the person needs love and forgiveness and someone to help them. I have found that, in order to build relationship with people from other races, you need to be willing to hang out in a group of people where you are not in the majority or where you are out of your depth.

If we are who we claim we are, we need to take on a Christlikeness, we need to value people and their respective cultures. We need to be unified in Christ and that really means swallowing your pride. Sometimes this means stepping into circles where you will be accused of things, but if you can slowly break down their perceptions of you by loving them, you have made strides of progress. It can be difficult, however. I have attended a number of transformational talks at university. At one they said that if you are white, male, Christian and straight, you're not allowed to talk at the meeting as your opinion is not valid because you have never been through a struggle and you haven't experienced what other people have experienced. Living in a society where you are meant to be an individual and your opinion is meant to be valid, this can be discouraging. So it's a bit of a hypocritical system, and in those situations you feel like your whole identity is attacked on every single front.

These people often mean well, but they don't know how to fix this mess. They are hurting and want to see change, so the quickest way to see change is by putting rules down. Instead, they should be focussing on changing people's hearts. It is about repentance, forgiveness, letting go and loving people in order to show them that you're really interested in them as a person and that you're not coming with your own prejudiced agendas.

Even though it's polarised at times, I still witness a lot of multiracial interaction, integration and love on the campus. I often see completely culturally and racially mixed groups of people having fun, laughing together and doing life together; and I am privileged to be in some of those circles. A by-product of all this racial polarisation, is that it forces people to talk about it. As long as there are those people who value multiracial friendships, there is a lot of hope.

BEING ANTI-RACIST

Many people on campus say that they are not racist, but I believe that we need to take it further than our own personal beliefs if we want our society to become properly integrated, multiracial and devoid of all the prejudice and hate. It is not enough not to be racist, you have to be anti-racist. In my context, if I am with other white people, I have to stand up if they are making racist comments and tell them that they are wrong. We cannot allow racist people — whether black or white — to propagate their views and remain unchecked. If nobody ever tells them differently, how are they going to change? Sometimes you have to stick your neck out there and risk it with your own people in order for progress to take place. Yet, we need to do it in love, helping them understand a better way, a Christ-like way.

WHEN YOU FIND PEOPLE WHO ARE DIFFERENT TO YOU IN ANY WAY, IT ADDS A RICHNESS TO YOUR LIFE THAT YOU WOULDN'T HAVE IF YOU JUST MINGLE WITH PEOPLE WHO ARE THE SAME AS YOU.

Acknowledging people's culture and upbringing is important. It's saying that I recognise the importance and the value of the way you were raised and the culture you were raised in. It is ultimately seeing the good in our flawed cultures and understanding the fact that a person is a person. It's not that black and white is not important, but ultimately what's important is the person, inside of a cultural context. Many young people struggle to know where their place is in South Africa today. I believe that the best thing we as young people can do is to go out of our comfort zones and do life with people who don't look like or sound like us; to value all people as made in God's image and to love them regardless of them being different from us.

/ABOUT

Thando Phello is 18 years old and currently in Matric. He lives at Home-Base, an African Havens project. African Havens is the social outreach arm of Every Nation Rosebank. Thando is currently exploring options for further studies after completing school.

Shaun Pearce, son of Roger and Nicola Pearce, is 19 years old. He is a student at the University of Stellenbosch, studying a B Com law degree. He is passionate about God's Kingdom and feels a calling to be a missionary in the Middle East.

"LET NO ONE DESPISE YOU FOR YOUR YOUTH, BUT SET THE BELIEVERS AN EXAMPLE IN SPEECH, IN CONDUCT, IN LOVE, IN FAITH, IN PURITY."

1 TIMOTHY 4:12

JOURNAL POINTS

1. What were the main learning points for you in this chapter?

2. Have you experienced deep rejection in your life? Have you forgiven those who have rejected you? If not, ask the Lord to help you forgive and ask other Christians to stand with you in this.

3. How do you see the future of South Africa? How can you grow to have more hope?

4. Are you stepping out of your comfort zones to cross the divide? How can you do this more?

5. Think about the term anti-racist. Can you go as far as to say that you are anti-racist? If not, ask the Lord to work in your heart on a deep level, so that you will be courageous in standing against racism whenever you encounter it.

CHAPTER TWELVE

PARLEZ-VOUS FRANÇAIS?

ROGER PEARCE

➤————→

"There are no ordinary people. You have never talked to a mere mortal. Nations, cultures, arts, civilizations — these are mortal, and their life is to ours as the life of a gnat. But it is immortals whom we joke with, work with, marry, snub and exploit — immortal horrors or everlasting splendours. This does not mean that we are to be perpetually solemn. We must play. But our merriment must be of that kind (and it is, in fact, the merriest kind) which exists between people who have, from the outset, taken each other seriously — no flippancy, no superiority, no presumption."

C.S. Lewis, The Weight of Glory

When South Africa's borders opened to immigrants from Africa in the early 1990s, there was a massive influx of people coming into the country from many African nations. Many were fleeing horrific situations such as the Rwandan genocide, war or extreme oppression and found accommodation in the inner cities of South Africa, places like Hillbrow in Johannesburg.

All of a sudden, there was a great number of French-speaking people from all over Africa living in our midst and coming to our churches. People like Michel, Jacques, Francois and Christine who could hardly speak English. Their cultures were completely foreign to us. We had to find ways to connect with them, and misunderstandings were the norm of the day. A classic example of this was our wedding. We invited only our closest friends to the wedding, of which included three of our new French friends. However, 25 of them decided to come. This was something unheard of in our culture, but very normal in theirs. For them it was a case of, "Of course we are coming to your wedding, we're so happy for you!" They didn't in their wildest dreams consider that they needed an invitation. Fortunately, we didn't have a sit-down meal, so the informal nature of our wedding could lend itself to more guests!

So began an awesome journey of getting to know each other. I started a small connect group in the notorious Hillbrow in the early 1990s. The connect group eventually grew to about 60 people. At one stage, we were running the group in Ponte, one of the most dangerous buildings in Johannesburg. It's a round skyscraper with apartments centred around a dark hole in the middle of the building. Time and time again, people would jump down into that abyss committing suicide, yet there was such life and light in our group. As we grew, we couldn't all fit properly into the apartment, so people would squeeze in, some sitting around the corner in the passage way, listening to the message and singing their hearts out.

Here were people who were fleeing desperate situations and finding God in a strange land. Their lives and their futures were being changed forever. I am sure my preaching was awful those days, but just the fact that they were being received and loved made them come by the dozens. I would preach my best sermon and be finished in about 20 minutes, but that was not enough. They would want more, saying a sermon should be an hour and a half long. I needed to adjust to their culture. I had a wonderful time of learning to sing French songs, preaching with an interpreter, being exposed to food like Kapenta (a type of small fish popularly eaten in countries like Zambia and Zimbabwe). Nicola and I loved sharing meals with them, sometimes at their place, sometimes at ours. We also went evangelising door to door in Hillbrow an hour before connect group. We gladly braved the streets of Hillbrow to walk to people's rooms and invite them to hear more about a God who loved them, and we were so well received because of it.

The connect group in Hillbrow eventually grew into two churches. The words of Pastor Michel Muloway (Every Nation Rosettenville) blessed me tremendously: "It was in 1992 when I personally saw a white man in Hillbrow. He was young and vibrant, not fearing the area but discipling anyone who he came in contact with. That was the first time we met Roger Pearce. He made us feel welcome and gave us hope in this new country. We soon enrolled at His People Bible School on Wits campus, completing it in the year 2000. Four years later, my wife and I started a ministry. Around the time that Roger became the Senior Pastor at His People, we joined our ministry to theirs. We were welcomed with open arms. Roger always made us feel secure, his care knew no boundaries and he accepted us for who we are. He is a real unifier of people. In the time of xenophobia, he came to encourage our church. May the Lord always bless Roger and all his family."

We got to know and love the foreigner, but many others began to see them more and more as a threat to local South Africans, mainly due to the perception of them taking local jobs. This lead to the tragic xenophobic crises we experienced in South Africa in recent history.

X E N O P H O B I A

The Southern African Migration Project (SAMP), reported that one of the by-products of South Africa's "open border" policy has been a growth in intolerance towards foreigners. Xenophobia, the deep-rooted, irrational hatred or fear directed towards foreigners or anything foreign, has become a huge problem in South Africa in recent years.

We have experienced two major xenophobic crises, the first in 2008 and then again as recent as 2015. Graphic pictures of South Africans brutally necklacing Zimbabwean refugees (attaching a burning tire around someone's neck) made front-page news worldwide in 2008. Over 100,000 people were displaced and at least 50 brutally murdered. In an article published in Joy!Digital, Dr Peter Hammond[9] mentions a Human Rights Watch report about a campaign known as Buyelekhaya (meaning "Go back home"), which blamed foreigners for unemployment. Some of the accounts Hammond cites in his article include:

- A Mozambican and two Senegalese were thrown out of a moving train by a group returning from a rally in Alexandra township that blamed foreigners for unemployment.

- Residents in Zandspruit in Johannesburg demanded that all Zimbabweans leave their area and then forcibly evicted them and burned down their homes.

- In Olievenhoutbosch, Zimbabweans were attacked and killed and their belongings set alight amidst demands by the locals that police remove all immigrants from the area. "These foreigners disrespect our culture, they don't speak our language, they take our women and they take our jobs!"

- Over 47 Somali refugees were murdered in two months as part of a campaign to drive Somali traders out of townships in the Western Cape. "These foreign people come to South Africa with nothing, but tomorrow he has cash, third day he owns a shop and fourth day he has a car. Where do these foreign people get this money from?"

- Local people attacked immigrants from Malawi, Zimbabwe and Mozambique, saying that foreigners were taking their jobs.

On 18 May 2015, a digital British newspaper, *The Week*, had the following to say about the latest xenophobic attacks in South Africa:

The latest outbreak of violence began last month in the coastal city of Durban and quickly spread to the financial hub of Johannesburg. Locals attacked foreigners, particularly targeting Malawians, Zimbabweans, Ethiopians and Mozambicans, in several townships in and around the city. Some of the victims were reportedly stabbed and one man was burned alive. Police used stun grenades, water cannons and rubber bullets to disperse the angry mob looting foreign-owned businesses, while owners were forced to arm themselves with machetes, axes and sticks ... Thousands of people have been displaced, seeking refuge at police stations, churches and temporary accommodation set up by NGOs. "Please help us. They want to kill us," Ethiopian shop owner Aka Bob Amaha told Times Live reporters. "We can't stay in our shops waiting for them to burn us."10

I knew people who were too scared to send their children to school during this time, others who were petrified of going to work or taking public transport to go to school or church. So many innocent people's lives, homes and jobs were in jeopardy. During these times of crisis, many churches and NGOs responded by creating places of refuge for those under attack. The His People church in Cape Town opened up its N1 City venue for people to stay in, spending their whole year's budget to feed them and meet their basic needs. In Johannesburg, we ran a tented camp close to Alexandra for displaced families. We helped thousands of people and even though it felt like organised chaos most of the time, it was so rewarding to be the hands and feet of Jesus to these people.

LOVE YOUR NEIGHBOUR AS YOURSELF

Xenophobia in South Africa has both socio-economic and sinful roots. We live in a society grappling with massive inequality, deep poverty and high unemployment. These are real issues touching millions of lives. Criminal elements then step in to piggy-back on these issues, using xenophobia as an excuse to steal from others. Lawlessness and violence is not the answer. Attacking the stranger in our midst is a terrible sin and we cannot simply ignore this crisis. God very clearly commands us to not do wrong to the stranger or alien among us. Indeed, we are exhorted to treat them as our "native-born".

The Bible says in Mark 12:30-31, "Love the Lord your God with all your heart and with all your soul and with all your mind and with all your strength … love your neighbour as yourself." The Christian response to xenophobia is to love our neighbour as ourselves, to do to them as we would want to be done unto ourselves — and to teach others to do the same.

Some might ask, "Who is my neighbour?" When Jesus was challenged by this potentially xenophobic question, he specifically chose a Samaritan, who was a foreigner despised by the Jews of his day as an example (Luke 10:29-37). However, prejudice makes loving our neighbour an impossible task. How are we supposed to love our neighbour if we keep our distance because of what we think is the truth, and what we have been taught is the norm? After all, closeness brings clarity, and clarity brings charity.[11]

EMBRACING BIBLICAL PRINCIPLES

God calls us not only to see lives saved, but to see communities transformed as we bring God's ways and will into all of society.

Equality before the law is very much a biblical principle that we are called to embrace. Numbers 15:15-16 states this very strongly, "The community is to have the same rules for you and for the alien living among you; this is a lasting ordinance for the generations to come. You and the alien shall be the same before the Lord. The same laws and regulations will apply both to you and to the alien living among you."

The Word of God frames our response to foreigners over and over:

- "You shall not wrong a stranger or oppress him, for you were strangers in the land of Egypt." (Exodus 22:21)

- "… if you do not oppress the alien, the fatherless or the widow, or shed innocent blood in this place, and if you do not go after other gods to your own hurt, then I will let you dwell in this place, in the land that I gave of old to your fathers for ever." (Jeremiah 6:6-7)

- "The foreigner residing among you must be treated as your native-born. Love them as yourself, for you were foreigners in Egypt. I am the LORD your God." (Leviticus 19:34)

It is our responsibility to see all people as created in God's image and to love the foreigner by welcoming them into our country and hearts. It is our personal responsibility to get to know others and to attempt to understand where they come from.

- Loving our neighbour means protecting them, caring for them and seeing them succeed.

- Love means that we do not remain silent nor turn a blind eye.

- Love means getting in there and helping out when people are under attack.

- Love means that we stand up for what is right and true.

- Love means that we show God's love into our communities and neighbourhoods and bring faith where there is fear, hope where there is despair and righteousness where unrighteousness prevails.

- Love means going the extra mile to understand someone else and to build bridges so that we can cross the divide and become "one in Christ".

THE RWANDAN GENOCIDE
AND OTHER ATROCITIES

In Rwanda, 1994 saw the murder of approximately 800 000 Rwandans in only three months. The Rwandan genocide was the mass killing of Tutsi and moderate Hutu civilians between April and June 1994, set against the backdrop of the Rwandan Civil War. This organised campaign of xenophobic violence was perpetrated by the Rwandan army and other government-backed militias. Hutu civilians were also called upon to murder their Tutsi acquaintances. Rwandan citizens were officially classified by whether or not they were Hutu, Tutsi or Twa. This classification could be seen on the identity cards and helped the Hutus identify the Tutsis. This system of ethnic discrimination led to the destruction of up to 70% of Rwanda's Tutsi population.

Distrust between the Tutsis and the Hutus stemmed from an engrained idea of ethnic superiority. Rwanda was originally a German colony. The colonisers favoured the Tutsis as they were taller and had lighter skin, thereby looking more European. The Tutsis, despite being a minority group, were put in roles of responsibility. However, as the Hutus gained leverage with Belgium, the new colonial power, newspapers and radio stations became involved in pro-Hutu propaganda and, eventually, in playing an active role in the genocide. By commanding Hutus to "cut down tall trees" and to "crush the cockroaches", the media succeeded in dehumanising the Tutsis. They became the scapegoats for the nation's problems. Through this, the media painted the slaughter as a necessary evil; something that must be done in order to rid the nation of "cockroaches". Current Rwandan President Paul Kagame comments that, "all genocides begin with an ideology – a system of ideas that says: This group of people here, they are less than human and they deserve to be exterminated."

This issue is not just an African one. For centuries and across continents, the notion of "the other" and "the foreigner" has been prevalent and has led to significant violence. In 2001, for example, tensions rose between the white majority and Southern Asian minority in Britain. The tension escalated into violent, ethnically-motivated riots in towns such as Bradford and Oldham. The Yugoslav Wars were a series of ethnic conflicts that were fought among the people of former Yugoslavia between 1991 and 2001. Approximately 140 000 people lost their lives as a result of violent acts in their effort to ethnically cleanse the population. Thousands of Bosnian women were systematically raped in order to achieve this ethnic cleansing. As recently as 2010, there has been violent action in southern Kyrgyzstan between ethnic Kyrgyz and Uzbeks. This violence stemmed from a history of distrust between the ethnic groups, including riots in the 1990s between the two groups that had led to a death toll of up to 1000 people.

"THERE IS NEITHER JEW NOR GREEK, THERE IS NEITHER SLAVE NOR FREE, THERE IS NO MALE AND FEMALE, FOR YOU ARE ALL ONE IN CHRIST JESUS."

GALATIANS 3:28

JOURNAL POINTS

1. What were the main learning points for you in this chapter?

2. Are you friends with someone from another African nation who is residing in South Africa at present? Have you taken time to understand their background and struggles?

3. How can we as individuals and as the church practically embrace the foreigner more? (For example, help facilitate understanding of each other through cultural evenings and shared meals.)

4. What can we do as individuals, families, schools or the church to help those who are currently experiencing threats or conflict due to their foreign nationality?

I Love My City

Photo credit: Talitha Neville

CHAPTER THIRTEEN

STEPPING OUT OF OUR CULTURAL SILOS

NICKY NEVILLE

➤

"Strength lies in differences, not in similarities."

Stephen R. Covey

A HEDGE OF BITTER ALMONDS

"TWO MINDS, TWO WORLDS,
ONE COUNTRY ... WHERE
PEOPLE OCCUPY THE SAME
SPACE BUT LIVE IN DIFFERENT
TIME FRAMES SO THAT THEY
DO NOT SEE EACH OTHER
AND PERCEIVE DIFFERENT
REALITIES."

—ALLISTER SPARKS

Long before Apartheid, a hedge of bitter almonds divided black and white people in South Africa. Allister Sparks in *The Mind of South Africa*, speaks about the hedge of bitter almonds that can still be seen in the beautiful Kirstenbosch Gardens in Cape Town today. This ancient hedge was planted in 1660 by Jan Van Riebeeck of the Dutch East India Company. Van Riebeeck, the leader of the first Dutch settlers to the Cape, had explicit orders that, "he was to barter cattle from the Khoikhoi to get fresh meat, but apart from that he and his small band of settlers were not to interact with them at all".[12]

Van Riebeeck planted a bitter almond hedge to seal off his community from the indigenous inhabitants of Africa. The hedge divided this small white community from the African continent stretching to the north, creating its own little enclave of Europe. In fact, Van Riebeeck was first instructed to dig a canal from Table Bay to False Bay that would have turned the Cape Peninsula into a European island literally cut off from Africa, but he felt that he didn't have the manpower to do this, so planted the hedge instead. As Sparks points out, "There is more to the bitter-almond hedge than what you see from where it grows". [13]

Apartheid, with its separation of white and black living areas, schools, social amenities, political institutions, trains, buses, taxis, hospitals and cemeteries, had its roots in a long-standing division first created by the early settlers to the Cape. Sparks continues, "...what is deeper than any of these is the division that runs through the psyche of the nation ... Two minds, two worlds, one country ... where people occupy the same space but live in different time frames so that they do not see each other and perceive different realities ." [14]

THIS HAS REIGNITED THE
DEBATE ABOUT RACE AND
ALSO THE REALISATION THAT
AS MUCH AS THE NATION
HAS MOVED ON, WE ARE STILL
DIVIDED.

Sparks wrote this book before the fall of Apartheid and although these external divisions created by the Apartheid system do not exist anymore, many South Africans still live in a divided world and continue to see life through these lenses. In fact, more than 20 years after our new democracy was founded, we continue to live in a divided country where race is still a key part of our national dialogue. In recent times, there has been a lot of attention on people making racist comments in the media or even in their personal capacity. This has reignited the debate about race and also the realisation that as much as the nation has moved on, we are still divided.

A VERY REAL DIVIDE

This is a book about stories. The story of very different people from very diverse cultures and backgrounds. It is our story as a nation. How is it possible for us to merge these stories into one? What is it that enabled the people featured in this book to cross the divide that exists between people groups in South Africa? How can we all get to a point where we can stand side by side in unity? In a country that has historically been so divided, where we have all held on to our own people for survival, how can we learn to, whilst honouring our own cultures, respect the cultures of others and together become a distinct new people?

CULTURE — A FINICKY THING

Ed Stetzer said, "The way we engage culture as Christ followers matters. It matters a lot." Let's first take a closer look at this finicky thing called culture. The Oxford Dictionary defines culture as, "The customs and beliefs, art, way of life and social organization of a particular country or group." [15]

Addressing issues of culture is a sensitive subject everywhere. In Culture Matters, respected economic historian David Landes says, "Yet, culture, in the sense of the inner values and attitudes that guide population, frightens scholars ... criticisms of culture cut close to the ego and injure identity and self-esteem. Coming from outsiders, such animadversions [strong criticisms], however tactful and indirect, stink of condescension ." [16]

If taking the issue of culture head on even frightens scholars, how can we as normal people living in South Africa today hope to understand this complex issue, let alone solve the problems of our nation?

HOW CAN WE LEARN TO, WHILST HONOURING OUR OWN CULTURES, RESPECT THE CULTURES OF OTHERS AND TOGETHER BECOME A DISTINCT NEW PEOPLE?

A Harvard Business School scholar said that, "Attitudes, values and beliefs that are sometimes collectively referred to as 'culture' play an unquestioned role in human behaviour and progress. This is evident to me from working in nations, states, regions, inner cities, and companies at widely varying stages of development. The question is not whether culture has a role, but how to understand this role..." [17]

GOOD AND BAD IN EVERY CULTURE

All people live in a culture of some sort. There is no neutral position, one that might allow a person to stand in a cultural vacuum and make objective pronouncements on the cultures of others. All people, whether they realize it or not, are shaped by the culture in which they live. In South Africa, our culture has been shaped by the stories we have been told growing up, our interactions with others, our education, social class and race. Essentially, our culture defines how we view ourselves and this view shapes how we see others and how we treat them, understand them and interact with them.

"ALMOST EVERY CULTURAL PHENOMENON HAS ASPECTS THAT CAN BE AFFIRMED BY SCRIPTURE, AS WELL AS ASPECTS THAT ARE IDOLATROUS DISTORTIONS OF THE TRUTH. TO ONLY FOCUS ON WHAT CAN BE AFFIRMED IS TO DULL THE PROPHETIC EDGE OF THE GOSPEL'S HARD TRUTH. TO ONLY FOCUS ON WHAT SHOULD BE CHALLENGED IS TO FAIL TO SHOW HOW THE CULTURE'S LONGINGS ARE ANSWERED IN JESUS."

— TREVIN WAX

Our cultures also shape our perception and reception of the Christian faith. Stetzer points out that culture itself is not evil, but "a composite of good and evil (as understood biblically) values and vocations, customs and creations, beliefs and behaviours that characterise a particular people in a particular place". [18]

We need to respect the fact that every culture, however fallen, reflects something of God. As Trevin Wax says, "Almost every cultural phenomenon has aspects that can be affirmed by Scripture, as well as aspects that are idolatrous distortions of the truth. To only focus on what can be affirmed is to dull the prophetic edge of the Gospel's hard truth. To only focus on what should be challenged is to fail to show how the culture's longings are answered in Jesus." [19]

So, if there is good and bad in every culture, how do we make sure that we don't throw the baby out with the bath water? How do we respect the culture of our fathers, learn to respect the culture of others and together embrace the culture of the Kingdom?

DOUBLE LISTENING

Our doctrine and theology can be excellent, but if we don't grasp the interests and longings of those around us or if we don't care, we will not be able to scratch where they itch. I cannot fully love my neighbours unless I understand them and the cultural world they inhabit.

Cultural literacy — the ability to understand our own culture and the cultures of those around us — is important if we wish to impact our world. When God became man He became a historically, culturally-conditioned man in a particular time and place. He was part of a particular culture and found ways to engage those around Him within this cultural context.

John Stott calls what Jesus practised double listening, "By double listening, I mean listening, of course, to God and to the Word of God, but listening to the voices of the modern world as well. Now, I make it clear that in listening to the modern world, we are not listening with the same degree of respect as that with which we listen to the voice of God. We listen to Him in order to believe and obey what He says. We listen to the modern world, not in order to believe and obey what it says, but in order to understand its cries of pain, the sighs of the oppressed. And it seems to me that relevant communication grows out of this process of double listening." [20] We are called to be people who double listen.

ENGAGING THE CULTURES OF OUR DAY

We cannot meaningfully engage people for the cause of Christ without such understanding. However, this is complicated by the world in which we live where we are encouraged to stand up for number one — me, myself and I. We are taught to express our opinions, but need to be taught to also listen to the voices of others so that we can truly understand them — their walk, their struggles, their history and their culture.

This means that we need to engage the cultures of the day and not run from them. Paul says that we are not called to "leave the world" (1 Corinthians 5:10), but rather to "become all things to all men" so as to engage them with the Gospel (1 Corinthians 9:22). Jesus often used illustrations in the Gospels from everyday life to connect with His audience. When it comes to speaking truth into the lives of

I BELIEVE THE KEY TO CONNECTING WITH THOSE OF OTHER CULTURES, IS TO STRIVE TO UNDERSTAND THEM AND HAVING UNDERSTOOD THEM, TO CONNECT WITH THEM AND THEN TO MOVE FORWARD TOGETHER.

people searching for it, we cannot do anything less. Rather than living just in our own Christian culture, we are called to seek to understand those around us, to hear their stories and to cross the divide between us and them, and to help them do the same.

Many of us have lived in cultural silos for a very long time, with very little understanding of each other. It has been safe remaining amongst those of the same culture, doing what we know, trusting what we are used to and giving into the fear of venturing out into the unknown. I believe the key to connecting with those of other cultures, is to strive to understand them and having understood them, to connect with them and then to move forward together.

"EVERY DAY YOU AND I ARE MAKING DECISIONS THAT HELP CONSTRUCT ONE KIND OF WORLD OR ANOTHER. ARE WE CO-OPTED BY THE FADDISH WORLDVIEWS OF OUR AGE, OR ARE WE HELPING TO CREATE A NEW WORLD OF PEACE, LOVE AND FORGIVENESS? HOW NOW SHALL WE LIVE? BY EMBRACING GOD'S TRUTH, UNDERSTANDING THE PHYSICAL AND MORAL ORDER HE HAS CREATED, LOVINGLY CONTENDING FOR THAT TRUTH WITH OUR NEIGHBOURS, THEN HAVING THE COURAGE TO LIVE IT OUT IN EVERY WALK OF LIFE."[21]

— CHARLES COLSON

/ABOUT

Dennis and Nicky Neville live in Johannesburg with their four daughters, Daniella, Talitha, Olivia and Tiffany. Nicky holds a Master's Degree in Organisational Leadership (specialising in Communications and Culture) from Regent University. Dennis also contributed to various chapters in this book. He was the head of the His People Bible Schools in South Africa, as well as the His People Institute that focussed on deeper thinking issues, such as worldviews and the role of Christianity in society. They currently head up a non-profit project called Home-Base, that provides orphaned and vulnerable youth with opportunities for tertiary studies after completing school; and they are launching a vocational training school in 2017.

"BEHOLD, HOW GOOD AND PLEASANT IT IS WHEN BROTHERS DWELL IN UNITY! IT IS LIKE THE PRECIOUS OIL ON THE HEAD, RUNNING DOWN ON THE BEARD, ON THE BEARD OF AARON, RUNNING DOWN ON THE COLLAR OF HIS ROBES! IT IS LIKE THE DEW OF HERMON, WHICH FALLS ON THE MOUNTAINS OF ZION! FOR THERE THE LORD HAS COMMANDED THE BLESSING, LIFE FOREVERMORE."

PSALM 133: 1-3

JOURNAL POINTS

1. What were the main learning points for you in this chapter?

2. List some aspects of your culture that you think are in line with the Bible and list some aspects of your culture that you think are not in line with biblical principles.

3. What experiences with different cultures have shaped you and the way you see others? How can you learn to accept their cultures as important and valid, even though they are different than yours?

4. How can we learn to double-listen? What does it entail?

5. How can we as Christians engage the culture of our day more effectively?

6. What has God called you to do to change your culture in a positive way?

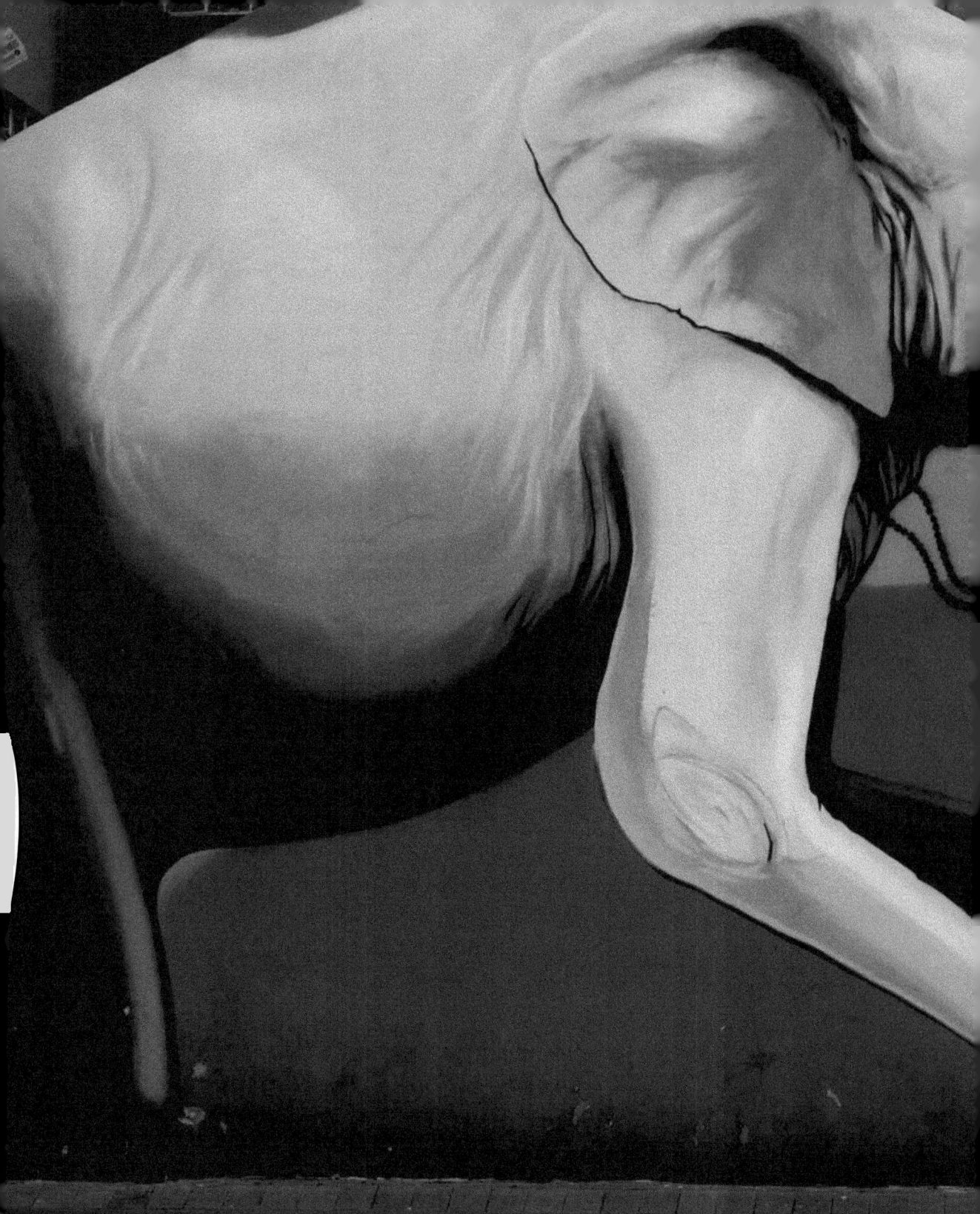

CHAPTER FOURTEEN

CROSSING THE DIVIDE

ROGER PEARCE

>——→

"We build too many walls and not enough bridges."

Isaac Newton

WHAT DO ALL OF THESE STORIES MEAN?

As you have read through the preceding chapters, my prayer is that you have started to understand both the complexity and the beauty that is South Africa. I am sure that, as you have read these stories, your heart has been touched and hopefully your thinking has been challenged.

We each have our own story. Every one of us who call South Africa home have encountered injustice and racism, in some way or another. We all continue to be impacted by the legacy of Apartheid. There are several common threads that stand out from the stories in this book.

- It has been heart-breaking to read the many accounts where people have shared about their experiences of deep hurt and rejection as children. I realised how the devil works at bringing hurt into young lives, in whichever way he can. As this hurt takes root in a person's heart, it often leads to unforgiveness and bitterness, which then ends up crippling the person both emotionally and spiritually.

- Many of the stories also outline the sense of injustice that people have experienced during the Apartheid years and afterwards. They have had to come to grips with the hurts and fears that our history of division and discrimination have caused. This sense of injustice has caused people to act and to respond in various ways.

- Another thread that flows through these stories is that people have emerged with the hope that things can get better — the realisation that although we are different, we are indeed better together.

- It has been clear that this journey to togetherness is not an easy one and is fraught with frustrations, emotions, hurts, fears and concerns about the future.

- Each person has come to recognise that in their own strength, they are not able to properly cope with these challenges. They have come to a place of recognising that they need God's hand, His grace and His mighty power to bring both the healing and the change that is needed.

- It is clear that the issues at hand are not just of laws or regulations. The Apartheid laws have been gone for over twenty years, but the divide still exists. It is clear that the solution is not merely a legal one or a regulatory one, but that true change also requires a heart change.

- There is a pervading hope for the future of this nation. In the heady days of 1994 and 1995, hope for the future of our nation was at a high point, but the passage of the years, the death of Nelson Mandela, the rise of corruption and the lack of change in so many areas have caused this hope to fade. However, there is still so much hope.

What is our solution? How do we, having travelled through these stories, step into the best future for our nation? What can we do to be better together?

WE ARE DIVIDED

First, we need to recognise the reality that we do live in a nation which is still very much divided. I have heard people say that "Apartheid is over … Let's stop looking back and let's move forward." This is a very shallow and naïve understanding of the realities of our nation and the deep chasm that has been created over decades, in fact over centuries. The laws may have changed, but many of the realities still exist in very real ways. We still live in a divided society.

We are still divided by race. We see the world through racial stereotypes and still judge people based on the colour of their skin. If you listen closely to what is happening in social media and on the news, you can see this division in stark ways, as people are still defined or described by the colour of their skin. We battle these constructs that have been entrenched in cultures and families for generations.

We are divided by culture. We are a nation of so many different cultures living alongside one another. People with British origins may look down on Afrikaans people, Zulus might feel superior to Sothos, Greeks sometimes look down on people from Cyprus, and on and on. These cultural differences create huge misunderstandings, which at times lead to increased racial tension. For example, in a recent conversation with a black member of our team he described going to a children's party. The white hosts had served up a few muffins and a plate of biltong (dried, slated meat) as eats. Sitting there he and his wife were feeling insulted as within their culture, visitors should be fed properly and he felt offended by the small amounts of snacks on offer. I had to explain that within our European culture, as it was not meal time, there was no expectation of serving a meal. Indeed, the fact that they were offered a more expensive treat in the form of biltong showed honour rather than an insult. These kind of 'small' issues can so quickly lead to racial tension as we fail to understand each other's culture.

We are divided by language. South Africa has 11 official languages and even more languages that are practiced on the ground. We thus not only often fail to understand one another's culture but this is exacerbated by our failure to understand what we are saying. For example, although English is widely used, it creates a division as those who can speak, read and write English find themselves with more opportunities that those who have not mastered English despite their full proficiency in one or more other languages.

All of these things impact the 54,995,390 residents of this beautiful nation and create large divisions between us.

WE HAVE INHERITED APARTHEID

We are the recipients of a very long legacy of seeing differences and of acting towards one another on the basis of this. These differences have been present in our society for so long that in many cases they have defined who we are. Apart from the Apartheid laws that undoubtedly played a major role in where we are today, history tells us that we have, in fact, been divided for hundreds of years.

These divisions have created a psychological impact with some people feeling superior and others inferior. The structural impact has been huge as the Apartheid government with their policies of separate development structurally and geographically separated the races. This means that even today 20 years after the end of Apartheid, black people still find it difficult to be accepted within traditionally white suburbs. The economic impact also continues to reverberate through our nation. As whites had more access to education and career opportunities, a large percentage of the wealthier individuals are still white and this is reflected in everything from the composition of corporate boards to property ownership. Indeed, we are called to pass on a legacy from one generation to the next, but millions of people who were not the right skin colour were denied this legacy. There are thus huge economic discrepancies.

As we look at all of the above, we can understand the growing sense of frustration in this nation, especially among the young people.

THE ROOT

At the root of this division is sin and fear. Sin separates and builds a barrier between us and God as well as between one another. Sin entered the world through the disobedience of Adam and Eve in the garden of Eden. We read in Genesis 1:27, "So God created man in his own image, in the image of God he created him; male and female he created them." We are all created in the image of God and we read that Adam and Eve walked with God in the Garden of Eden.

However, in Genesis 3:1b, 5, we see that the serpent spoke to Eve saying, "Did God actually say you shall not eat of any tree in the garden? ... For God knows that when you eat of it your eyes will be opened, and you will be like God knowing good and evil." Look carefully at this Scripture — Adam and God were walking together in the garden. However, the serpent came in and brought division. He questioned what God had said and he put seeds of doubt and distrust into their relationship. Adam and Eve then gave in to the temptation of the serpent and ate of the forbidden fruit. Their sin of disobedience to God opened the door to division entering our world. Not only did sin separate them from God (they were banished from the garden of Eden and could no longer walk in close relationship with God because of their sin), but sin separated them from each other (Adam blamed Eve for listening to the serpent and they even ended up having to kill an animal to create a covering for their nakedness). Sin created division.

It is the same today. Sin creates division between us, as our sinful nature would have us blame the other person for our lot in life. Rather than taking responsibility for our own life, owning our own part in all this, we tend to cast blame on others, our society, other races and so on. Sin still separates us from God and from each other. Division is the trick of the enemy. He seeks to create a divide between us and God and between every one of us. The fruit of this sin in our lives today are anger, resentment, a culture of blame and envy of one another.

One key fruit of sin is fear. Sin has removed the safety of the garden. We now live in a world where we fear one another, we fear loss, we fear for the future and we fear death. Indeed, from South Africa's earliest days fear has been the wedge that has separated. Fear caused Van Riebeeck to build the hedge of bitter almonds around the Cape. Fear of others caused the Apartheid powers to set all of the laws in place that would segregate the population.

A song by the South African band, Bright Blue (more recently sung by Josh Groban), summed up this fear in the following words:

I knew a man who lived in fear
It was huge, it was angry, it was drawing near
Behind his house, a secret place
Was the shadow of the demon he could never face
He built a wall of steel and flame
And men with guns, to keep it tame

Then standing back, he made it plain

That the nightmare would never ever rise again

But the fear and the fire and the guns remain

It doesn't matter now

It's over anyhow

He tells the world that it's sleeping

But as the night came round

I heard its lonely sound

It wasn't roaring, it was weeping

This song, speaking about the walls that the Apartheid government built to protect themselves, and white people in general, well illustrates the impact of this fear. This fear, as reflected in the Apartheid machine, looked big and ugly from the outside, but in the end this fear was not roaring, but was weeping. This fear continues to echo through our nation today. Fear of others causes people to react with xenophobic violence. Fear of the future causes people to pull back into their racial or cultural silos.

Fear for the future rests like a dark, gray mist over many people in our nation today.

JESUS —
THE BRIDGE ACROSS THE DIVIDE

There is hope. We see so much division, but there is hope for a better picture. Nelson Mandela, in his inaugural speech at the Union Buildings in Pretoria on 10 May 1994, as South Africa entered its first month after the fall of Apartheid, said, "The time for the healing of the wounds has come. The moment to bridge the chasms that divide us has come. Never, never and never again shall it be that this beautiful land will again experience the oppression of one by another and suffer the indignity of being the skunk of the world. Let freedom reign. The sun shall never set on so glorious a human achievement!"

This sentiment of hope has dimmed over the last few years, but still remains like a thread running through the hearts of every person in this nation. But, how do we bridge the divide? How do we move our nation back to a sense of hopefulness rather than fear about our future? By building a bridge.

In our nation, we built bridges many different ways, by putting organisations and policies in place such as the Truth and Reconciliation Commission, Black Economic Empowerment and Broad Based Black

Economic Empowerment. None of these interventions, despite them having some measure of success, have been the complete answer.

Ancient bridges were often built in an arch, with the stones fitting together. A keystone was the wedge-shaped piece of stone at the apex of the stone arch. It is the final piece placed during construction but it is a crucial piece as it locks all of the other stones into position and allows the arched bridge to bear weight. Our challenge in South Africa is that we have had a lot of the right stones — all of the above, the life and vision of Nelson Mandela, great passion for our nation, and lots more — but we need a keystone.

This keystone is the person of Jesus Christ. Indeed, the Bible talks about this in Acts 4:11 which reads, "This Jesus is the stone that was rejected by you, the builders, which has become the cornerstone." God, in the person of Jesus Christ, wants to be present in our nation and is the keystone or cornerstone that will allow for the bridge to be built and the chasm between us to be healed. We know that Jesus came to rescue us from sin. Already, through His death on the Cross and His resurrection, He has bridged the divide between life and death. Jesus is our solution — His presence and action in this nation is what will serve as the keystone, and is what will provide a solid bridge that people will cross, which will bear the weight of the past, help us to deal with the challenges of the present and enable us to grow and prosper in the future.

WHAT SHOULD WE DO?

God uses us as individuals to be the salt and light within this nation. He has called us to be His hands and feet and to represent His heart here on earth. What then are we to do?

God has called us to:

1. Be bridge-builders:

We are called to look for ways to cross the divide and to be at the front of the battle in bridging it. This is not an area that we can or should be quiet about. Building a bridge is never an easy task. It requires both sides to give up and to move beyond their own hurts, anger, frustrations and fears. We need to recognise that reaching across the divide, although painful and messy, will build a bridge for our children's children. The alternative is a nation of walls and wars.

Remember the words of 2 Chronicles 7:14 which states, "If my people who are called by my name humble themselves, and pray and seek my face and turn from their wicked ways, then I will hear from heaven and will forgive their sin and heal their land." This divide can be bridged, but not in our own strength. It can be bridged through God's mighty power working through us. We are required to humble ourselves, to pray for our nation, to seek God's face and His vision for this land and to turn from our wicked ways. God then promises to heal our land.

What can you do today to build a bridge across one of these divides? What can you do to humble yourself? What wicked ways should you be turning away from?

2. Inspire hope

Antoine de Saint-Exupery said, "If you want to build a ship, don't drum up people to collect wood and don't assign them tasks and work, but rather teach them to long for the endless immensity of the sea." We need to be people that are continually casting the vision of the South Africa that we want to see.

Nelson Mandela, famously gave us a picture of the preferable future in his words spoken in 1964 at the Rivonia Trial, "I have fought against white domination, and I have fought against black domination. I have cherished the ideal of a democratic and free society in which all persons live together in harmony and with equal opportunities."

Although hope for this vision of South Africa has waned over the past years for some, God wants us to be people who are inspiring hope. In Jeremiah 29:11, God reminds us, "For I know the plans I have for you, declares the Lord, plans for welfare and not for evil, to give you a future and a hope."

What can you do today to inspire hope? What words can you use to inspire others with the hope of a better future?

3. Listen deeply

I am sure that the stories in this book have opened up your mind and heart to the stories, struggles and perspectives of others. To move forward as a nation and as individuals, we need to be listening deeply to these stories. We need to hear the cries of the heart. We need to meet lies with the truth. We need to listen deeply with the heart to truly understand one another. An African proverb says, "Sugarcane is sweetest at its joint". Listen for the sweetness. Listen, not to be right, but listen with the goal to understand.

What can you do to listen more deeply? What conversations do you need to have where you just keep quiet and listen?

4. Connect fully

It is easy in our busy times to live past one another. It is easier to stay within our cultural, social, racial and language silos. South Africa today is marked by superficial connections. We are polite with people of other races, we work with people of other races, but we often do not truly connect. We need to stop allowing fear, anger and hurt to keep us apart. Instead, we need to strive to connect in a real way. We need to see deep connections, where we share hearts, as worlds we can discover rather than as jungles we should avoid.

What conversations can you have to connect with someone who is different to you? Who can you invite into your home and into your life to connect with in a deeper way?

5. Seek to understand

"If you want to walk fast, walk alone. If you want to walk far, walk together." This African proverb sums up the hearts that we need to have. We need to recognise the power in walking together, in understanding one another and in being on this journey together as Africans. 2 Corinthians 5:16-17 says, "From now on, therefore, we regard no one according to the flesh. Even though we once regarded Christ according to the flesh, we regard him thus no longer. Therefore, if anyone is in Christ, he is a new creation. The old has passed away; behold, the new has come." We look beyond the outward, to the heart. We need to take the time to "get" people. We are not called to boast in our own achievements or those of our particular culture or race, but rather in the fact that we know the Almighty God and share a common journey as His children.

What can you do today to try to understand someone who is different? What difficult conversation must you have to clear up a dispute or to understand more of what you see through your own cultural lenses?

6. Forgive one another

God calls us to forgive one another and to spread the message of forgiveness. Martin Luther King Jnr said that "Darkness cannot drive out darkness; only light can do that. Hate cannot drive out hate; only love can do that." Forgiveness is an act of our will. We decide to hold something against someone else. We decide to let a bad seed grow. The seedbed for evil and anger and racism is unforgiveness. Choose to forgive. In Matthew 6:14-15 we are exhorted to forgive, "For if you forgive others their trespasses, your heavenly father will also forgive you, but if you do not forgive others their trespasses, neither will your father forgive your trespasses." Forgive.

Who do you need to forgive? Think of specific people that you need to forgive. Perhaps there is a particular race or culture that you need to forgive. Actively make the choice to forgive them today.

7. Repent

We are called to repent for the sins of those who have gone before us. Often, the easy route is to say, "But I was not there! I did not set the Apartheid laws in place!" or "I am not the one who committed those evil acts". God, however, calls us to repent for the sins of our fathers. In Nehemiah 9:2 we read, "And the Israelites separated themselves from all foreigners and stood and confessed their sins and the iniquities of their fathers." Jeremiah cried out to God in Jeremiah 14:20 saying, "We acknowledge our wickedness, O Lord, and the iniquity of our fathers, for we have sinned against you.". In this nation we have allowed the evil of racism to take root. We need to repent for the sins of our fathers.

We are also called to repent for our own sins. In Acts 3:19 we read, "Repent therefore and turn back, that your sins may be blotted out, that times of refreshing may come from the presence of the Lord." We need times of refreshing as individuals, but also as a nation. Let us together repent for the way we have treated one another, for the hurt we have caused, for our anger and for our hatred. Let's trust God for His refreshing and presence to flow through this nation.

What sins of your forefathers do you need to repent for? Who have they oppressed? What seeds have they sown in this nation? What do you personally need to repent of? How have you personally contributed to the oppression or notions of inferiority of people? Have you kept quiet instead of standing up for righteousness?

8. Put God at the centre in all that we do

Charles Spurgeon once challenged an audience, "Cast away your sloth, your lethargy, your coldness, or whatever interferes with your chaste and pure love for Christ, your soul's husband. Make Him the source, the centre, and the circumference of all your soul's range of delight." We need to recognise that we cannot change our society without Christ. We cannot hope to build the bridge without the keystone. We need to put God at the centre of all that we do. In John 15:5 we read the words of Jesus, "I am the vine; you are the branches. Whoever abides in me and I in him, he it is that bears much fruit for apart from me you can do nothing." In Matthew 6:33, we read, "But seek first the Kingdom of God and his righteousness, and all these things will be added to you." We need to place God at the centre and make sure that as we work to build this nation we are abiding in the vine.

What can you do to place God at the centre of your life? What habits can you set in place to ensure that Christ and not you is the centre of how you live and act?

9. Make disciples

In Matthew 28:19 Jesus commands us, "Go therefore and make disciples of all nations, baptising them in the name of the Father and of the Son and of the Holy Spirit, teaching them to observe all that I have commanded you." Discipleship is a core value of our Every Nation family. God has called us to make disciples of the nations. We need to work together to lead people to Christ and then walk with them in accountable relationships, teaching them to obey God in their lives. We need to be walking alongside people, helping them to find healing in God, challenging them in wrong, unbiblical mind-sets and equipping them to live victorious Christian lives.

We are called to not only disciple individuals, but to disciple nations. In Matthew 5:13-16 Jesus tell us, "You are the salt of the earth, but if salt has lost its taste, how shall its saltiness be restored? It is no longer good for anything except to be thrown out and trampled under people's feet. You are the light of the world. A city set on a hill cannot be hidden. Nor do people light a lamp and put it under a basket, but on a stand, and it gives light to all in the house. In the same way, let your light shine before others, so that they may see your good works and give glory to your father who is in heaven." We are called to impact our society by bringing God's rule and reign into our world. If we are each walking in obedience to God and His Word and bringing His truth into the area of life God has called us to, our society will be changed. God's light will be revealed and the salt of His Word will bring healing.

Do you have people in your life who can walk the journey with you and help you to find healing from the past? Are you walking in a discipling relationship with someone else? What can you do to bring light into the area of society God has called you to?

10. Love one another

In Genesis 1:27 we read, "So God created man in his own image, in the image of God he created him, male and female he created them." Each one of us carry the image of God in us. We reflect the image of God. A key challenge in the history of this nation is that we have not recognised this truth. As people, all created in the image of God, we all stand before God the same. We may have different colours, cultures and languages, but we are all equally valuable before God. There is no one who is better than another one. By hurting and harming those of another race, culture or language, we are sinning against God. Let us work to treat one another — no matter our race, language, culture or gender — as children of God. Jesus, in John 13:34-35 said these words, "A new commandment I give to you, that you love one another: just as I have loved you, you also are to love one another. By this all people will know that you are my disciples, if you have love for one another."

WHAT CAN YOU DO TODAY TO LOVE ONE ANOTHER?

Let's be the ones who build the bridges, with Jesus as the keystone, and usher in South Africa's next season. We are truly better together.

JOURNAL POINTS

1. From all that you have read in this book, what elements of these stories have impacted you the most?

2. Take time now to write down some firm commitments that you will make so that we become better together.

Action Step 1:

I will _____

Action Step 2:

I will _____

Action Step 3:

I will _____

Action Step 4:

I will _____

Action Step 5:

I will _____

Photo credit: Star & Harbour Photography

Photo credit: Star & Harbour Photography

DUNOON

We live in peace, we're covered,
Our places worlds apart
Brick walls, and food, a shower,
No fear or broken heart.

Panic is not our portion
If we will lose our lives
Calling in. No work today
comes as no surprise.

We're quick to sit in judgement.
More protest action on
What is it with 'these people'
Just let it all be gone.

We do not raise a finger
Or really show we care
We perpetuate what we know and love.
Is it not time to share?

Inertia and fear be gone!
Make that call and do
Listen to the needs out there
Be quick to follow through.

Time. It doesn't wait for us
So take it by the hand
Listen up and make a change
We need to shift like sand

We need to see what must be done
Oh Lord give us the grace
To hear your call, to give our time.
Help us to run this race.

People out there are waiting
To see if it is true
That the Christ we're following
Lives in me and you.

Lynne van Coller
25th April 2016. Copyright reserved.

REFERENCES

1. Hector Pieterson. (n.d.). Retrieved 8 March 2016 from https://en.wikipedia.org/wiki/HectorPieterson and from http://overcomingapartheid.msu.edu/image.php?id=65-254-1E

2. The Algerian War, also known as the Algerian War of Independence or the Algerian Revolution was a war between France and the Algerian National Liberation Front from 1954 to 1962, which led to Algeria gaining its independence from France. Algerian War (n.d.). Retrieved on 20 June 2016 from https://en.wikipedia.org/wiki/Algerian_War

3. Gallo, C. (2016). The Storyteller's Secret. New York: St. Martin's Press. p. 4.

4. Retrieved 17 April 2016 from http://www.sahistory.org.za/organisations/united-democratic-front-udf

5. Sanay, I. (n.d.). Madiba is gone; The struggle continues. Retrieved 6 February 2016 from www.panjab.org.uk/english/Madiba%20Is%20Gone.html; and from http://www.anc.org.za/show.php?id=206

6. A Short History of Coloured People in South Africa. (n.d.). Retrieved 6 June 2016 from http://v1.sahistory.org.za/pages/hands-on-classroom/classroom/pages/projects/grade12/lesson1/coloured-history.htm

7. Afrikaner Weerstandsbeweging. (n.d.). Retrieved 8 June 2016 from https://en.wikipedia.org/wiki/Afrikaner_Weerstandsbeweging

8. University of Fort Hare. (n.d.). Retrieved 24 May 2014. https://en.wikipedia.org/wiki/University_of_Fort_Hare

9. Hammond, P. (2015). A Christian Response to Xenophobia. Retrieved 27 June 2016 from http://www.joydigitalsa.com/news/a-christian-response-to-xenophobia/

10. South African Xenophobia – Why is there is much hatred of foreigners. (18 May 2015). Retrieved 27 June 2016 from http://www.theweek.co.uk/63378/south-african-xenophobia-why-is-there-so-much-hatred-of-foreigners

11. Quotable Quotes from Kagame's Speech. (9 April 2014). Retrieved 23 May 2016 from http://www.newvision.co.ug/new_vision/news/1339498/quotable-quotes-kagames-speech#sthash.1GSPmlSH.dpuf; Rwanda: How the Genocide happened. (17 May 2011). Retrieved 6 June 2016 from http://www.bbc.com/news/world-africa-13431486; The Rwandan Genocide. (n.d.). Retrieved 5 June 2016 from http://endgenocide.org/learn/past-genocides/the-rwandan-genocide/

12. Sparks, A. (1990). The Mind of South Africa. New York: Alfred A. Knopf. pp. xv.

13. Sparks, A. (1990). The Mind of South Africa. New York: Alfred A. Knopf. pp. xvii.

14. Sparks, A. (1990). The Mind of South Africa. New York: Alfred A. Knopf. pp. xvii.

15. Oxford Advanced Learners Dictionary. (2010). International Student's Edition. Oxford: Oxford University Press. pp. 357.

16. Landes, D. (2000). 'Culture makes all the difference.' in Harrison, L.E. & Huntington, S.P. Culture Matters. New York: Basic Books. pp. 2.

17. Porter, M.E. (2000). 'Attitudes, values, beliefs and the micro economics of prosperity.' in Harrison, L.E. & Huntington, S.P. Culture Matters. New York: Basic Books. pp. 14

18. Stetzer, E. (2014). What is Contextualization? Presenting the Gospel in Culturally Relevant Ways. Retrieved 19 April 2016 from www.christianitytoday.com/edstetzer/2014/october/what-is-contextualization.html

19. Wax, T. (2016). From Stephen Colbert to Taylor Swift: 4 Reasons I Write Cultural Commentary. Retrieved 19 April 2016 from https://blogs.thegospelcoalition.org/trevinwax/2016/01/14/from-stephen-colbert-to-taylor-swift-4-reasons-i-write-cultural-commentary/

20. Stott, R.W. (1997). Relevant biblical preaching: the art of double listening. Retrieved 19 April 2016 from www.ministrymagazine.org/archive/1997/01/relevant-biblical-preaching-the-art-of-double-listening

21. Colson, C. & Pearcey, N. (1999). How Now Shall we Live? Wheaton: Tyndale House Publishers. pp. 487.

www.ingramcontent.com/pod-product-compliance
Lightning Source LLC
LaVergne TN
LVHW061305060426
835513LV00013B/1244